TRUMPERICKS 2

TRUMPERICKS 2

"Stable Genius"

To Ivan — My future collaborator. Thanks + enjoy!
Best,
Bob Stone

ROBERT M. STONE

Illustrated by Chris Critelli

Copyright © 2018 Doggerel Enterprises, LLC
All rights reserved.

ISBN-13: 9781726337175
ISBN-10: 1726337170

For Nancy, David, Rachael, Jeni, Ryan, Kayla, Isabelle and Milo, who inspire, encourage and sustain me.

                                                                                 R.M.S.

The art in this book is humbly dedicated to my loved ones, who make it all worth it all. And to people everywhere who speak truth to power, and hold accountable the powerful.

                                                                                 C.B.C.

AUTHOR'S PREFACE

With the daily deluge of delirium from Trump-land, this sequel to "Trumpericks – A Doggerel Journey through the Twisted Mind of Donald Trump" practically wrote itself. It became a cleansing ritual for me; a form of therapy to vent my growing anger, frustration and fear over what this ignorant, arrogant narcissist is doing to undermine our democratic ideals and institutions, our social safety nets, the environment, the judiciary, race relations and general civility. Like the first volume, this compendium of limericks chronologically tracks events in rhyme, usually from Trump's unhinged point of view, with occasional appearances from his bumbling and bizarre supporting cast. Also like the first book, endnotes supply context for the verses. Together, the two books provide a comprehensive satirical history of the first 20 months of a presidency that, one hopes, will someday be considered a brief and aberrant episode that failed to cause lasting damage to our country and the world.

Again, I want to give sincere thanks to my family and friends who've supported this project with encouraging words and helpful ideas. Very special thanks go to Chris Critelli, an outstanding young man of many talents, who produced the clever artistic renderings that accompany my rhymes. And a shout-out to Crystal Bakhaj, who was indispensable in helping me solve the mysteries of word processing.

Here's to working our way back toward sanity through the 2018 midterm elections, the Mueller investigation, a free press willing to stand up to tyrants, and a more motivated and informed American electorate.

Bob Stone
Los Angeles, September 2018

NOTE FROM THE ILLUSTRATOR

Illustrating this book was both easy and not easy. It was easy because drawing is super fun. So most of the time, that work didn't feel too worky. It's also great collaborating with Bob, whom I have thank for his wit, whim, big heart, and steadfast work chronicling the highs, lows, and lower-stills that have punctuated and permeated these past months. So that part was a cinch.

Making this book was tough because, well, reality television has become a reality. And sometimes it feels like we're all strapped to our seats, squirming in the live-studio audience. So to revisit, scandal by scandal, outrage by outrage, national embarrassment by national embarrassment, the events of this past year – the reruns if you will – in an effort to comprehend and caricature them, required an emotional investment that was often heavy and exhausting.

That being said, it was worth it. I'm proud of the work in this book. This second time around the art is bigger, bolder, and explores a wider cast of characters. For as the swamp rises, so must we.

I'm also proud of the utility I hope these pages will have in the future. Years from now, once this chaotic time is in the rear-view-mirror and we're, hopefully, living in the light of the lessons we've learned, we can crack open this book, meticulously end-noted by Bob, and look back in astonishment at how very real all this was, and how dire it felt to live through it.

Here's to lessons learned.

I hope you have fun with our book!

Chris Critelli
NYC, September 2018

CONTENTS

WIKILEAKS	1
JUDGE ROY MOORE	1
MORE ROY MOORE	2
POST-THANKSGIVING BRAIN CRAMPS	3-4
"YOLK" OF AUTHORITARIANISM	5
MOORE, GILLIBRAND, HARASSMENT AND TAXES	5-7
CDC WORD POLICE	7-8
TAX "REFORM	9
DEEP FREEZE	10-11
HAVE A SAFE FLIGHT	12-13
MY NUKE BUTTON	14-15
DOING GRAMMAR (AND EVERYTHING ELSE) PROPER	16
STABLE GENIUS	16-17
FIRE AND FURY	18
SHITHOLE COUNTRIES	19
STORMY	19
GOVERNMENT SHUTDOWN	20-21
I'VE GOT THOSE INVESTIGATION BLUES	22
NUNES MEMO	23
AMERICAN DISGRACE (AND BAD SPELLER)	24-25
TREASON	26
I LOVE A PARADE	27
BEAT YOUR WIFE, GET A WHITE HOUSE JOB	28-29
WAITING IN THE WINGS	30-31
NO INTELLIGENCE HERE	32-33
PARKLAND, FLORIDA	34
MORE PARKLAND, FLORIDA	34-35
MORE INDICTMENT EXCITEMENT	36
PARKLAND, FLORIDA REVISITED	37
PENNSYLVANIA GERRYMANDERING	38
PARKLAND, FLORIDA AGAIN	39
LOSING HOPE	40
SESSIONS!	41
TARIFFS	42
LYING	42-43
BEN CARSON'S FURNITURE	44
NUNBERG	44
COHN RESIGNATION	45
CHAOS AND TURNOVER	45-47
BACK PEDDLING ON GUN CONTROL	48
FED UP WITH REX	48-49

MORE ON (MORON) REX	50
STAFF PARANOIA	50-51
MORE MUELLER TIME	52
THUNDERCLOUDS ON THE HORIZON	52
PUTIN ON THE RITZ	53
TARIFFS ON CHINA	54
BYE BYE H.R.	54-55
IMMIGRANT CARAVANS	56-57
ANOTHER BUSY WEEK	57-58
PRUITT BLEW IT	58-59
IT'S MY LAWYER'S FAULT!	60
BLAZING TOWER	60-61
THEY RAIDED MY LAWYER!	61-62
COMEY AND SCOOTER	63-64
RUDY FRUITY	64-65
ZTE AND ME	66
MISSING THE GOOD OLE DAYS	66-67
SUMMIT FEVER	67-68
JACK JOHNSON	69
A TRUMPIAN COMMENCEMENT SPEECH	70-72
PUTTING THE "ME" IN MEMORIAL DAY	73
ROSEANNE GETS BARRED	74-75
SPYGATE	75-76
CARNAC	77
PARDON ME!	78
GOD BLESS AMERICA!	79
SEPARATING FAMILIES	80-81
WATER BOTTLE PROTOCOL	82
DIPPY DIPLOMACY/DUMB-IT SUMMIT	82
G-7 SUMMIT	83
SINGAPORE FLING	84-85
MORE LOVE IN SINGAPORE	86
EXONERATION (NOT)!	87
INFESTATION	87-88
FOX NEWS PEANUT GALLERY	88-89
REVERSAL	89
MELANIA'S JACKET	90-91
BANNING MUSLIMS	92
DON'T SPARE THE ROD (OR MUELLER)	93
PRUITT DEPARTS (IN STEERAGE)	94
TAN BAN	94
MANCHURIAN CANDIDATE (AND PRESIDENT)	95-96

STRZOK, MUELLER, MAY, THE QUEEN, AND PUTIN	97
SO MANY NAMES!	98-99
NO MINYAN IN FINLAND	99-100
COLLUSION? NOT AN ILLUSION!	100
WORDSMITH	101
RECRUITIN' FOR PUTIN	102
CAPITAL IDEA	103
SUMMER CLEARANCE	104
DESTROYER LAWYER	104-105
HISTORIC DISTORTIONS	106
"ENEMY OF THE PEOPLE"	107
LEBRON	108
CALIFORNIA WILDFIRES	109-110
SPACE FARCE	110-111
OMAROSA	112-113
GIULIANI'S THEORY OF TRUTH RELATIVITY AND CONWAY'S COROLLARY	114
MUELLER AND MCCARTHY	114
BAD DAY AT BLACK ROCK	115-116
FLIPPERS	117
PECKER	117
WEISSELBERG	118
DISDAIN FOR MCCAIN	118-119
FUDGE!	120
IN THE ROUGH	120
FREE PASS FOR GOP CANDIDATES	121
INSIDER SHADING	122
HOW TO EXPLAIN A HURRICANE	123
A SEX PREDATOR'S UNINFORMED ADVICE TO WOMEN	123-124
TRUMPERY RHYMES	125-130
ENDNOTES	131-156

WIKILEAKS[1]
NOVEMBER 14, 2017

Our collusion was fast and footloose.
Now they're starting to tighten the noose.
It becomes somewhat sticky
when the leaks are from Wiki,
and the source of the intel is Russe.

JUDGE ROY MOORE[2]
NOVEMBER 14, 2017

When I served as the local D.A.,
I sought teen girls to hop in the hay.
Used my smooth southern drawl
in the old Gadsden Mall,
till they banned me from stalking my prey.

It was my job to put away crooks,
but I really liked fresh teenaged looks.
So I'd offer a ride
with some sex on the side.
Then I'd sign in their high school yearbooks.

None had yet reached an age to be weddable,
but I found them deliciously edible.
I'm a man of the Bible,
so their claims must be libel.
And, of course, as a judge I'm more credible.

Now I want to be Senator Moore.
There's no reason those efforts to score
with a temptress or five,
who were too young to drive,
should send my career on a detour.

MORE ROY MOORE
NOVEMBER 15, 2017

I embrace evangelical creed –
loving scripture in word and in deed.
But if you're a cute minor,
check out my new recliner.
A quick fondle is all that I need.

I took on the high court of our land,
to ensure all could read God's command.
You must follow His way:
not be Muslim or gay.
Want your crotch rubbed? I'll lend you my hand.

What's so wrong with a little flirtation
that evolves into child molestation?
It might seem out of bounds
to be stalking playgrounds.
But for me it's a privilege of station.

POST-THANKSGIVING BRAIN CRAMPS
NOVEMBER 29, 2017

Native veterans I came to extol,
but was lacking in impulse control:
Had to blurt, "Pocahontas,"
when what staffers don't want is
more Trump turds in the White House punch bowl.[3]

Needed Nancy and Chuck for some dealing,
so I fostered collegial feeling –
Sent a nasty false tweet.
Now they don't want to meet!
And the GOP leaders are reeling.[4]

What they might have been teaching at Wharton
is for allies it's best to go courtin'.
But if that's what they said,
it went over my head.
My attention span there was a short one.
(Now they're wondering what I've been snortin'.)

In this freakish reality show,
progress toward my agenda is slow.
So I try to distract,
use alternative fact,
imply murder committed by Joe.[5]

It's such fun using my Twitter feed
to attack people based on their creed.
I retweet alt-right rants,
fueling xenophobe chants.
Don't blame me if you see Muslims bleed.[6]

"YOLK" OF AUTHORITARIANISM[7]
DECEMBER 8, 2017

The oppressed masses don't have a "yolk"?
Guess somehow I am missing the jolk.
Since I hired the dregs,
we'll keep on laying eggs.
We can't spell and we're not so well-spolk.

PROCLAMATIONS

President Donald J. Trump Proclaims December 10, 2017, as Human Rights Day; December 15, 2017, as Bill of Rights Day; and the week beginning December 10, 2017, as Human Rights Week

Issued on: December 8, 2017

★ ★ ★

During Human Rights Day, Bill of Rights Day, and Human Rights Week, we rededicate ourselves to steadfastly and faithfully defending the Bill of Rights and human rights. Our God-given, fundamental rights are soon overcome if not safeguarded by the people. We, therefore, also reflect upon the many individuals who are unable to enjoy the God-given rights that we as Americans know are secure. We remember those suffering under the yolk of authoritarianism and extremism for doing nothing more than standing up to injustice or daring to profess or practice their religion, and we acknowledge those imprisoned or in peril simply because of their political views or their sex.

MOORE, GILLIBRAND, HARASSMENT AND TAXES
DECEMBER 14, 2017

As one sex predator to another,
I embraced Judge Roy Moore as my brother.
But the voters were strong:
sorted out right from wrong –
wouldn't let their morality smother.

Roy now staunchly declines to concede.
He laments that black slaves have been freed
to give Doug Jones their vote
and a victory of note.
It's this old South mind-set that we need.[8]

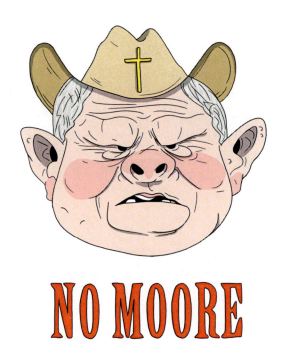

Overrated Kirsten Gillibrand
had the nerve to bite me on the hand.
Since that makes me real sore,
I'll imply she's a whore.
It's a tack that plays well in Trump-land.[9]

All my woman accusers have lied.
Why would unbiased folks take their side?
Harvey, Bill, Matt and Al
harassed many a gal.
For such conduct I'm too dignified.
(*Access Hollywood* comments aside.)[10]

My new tax plan is gonna be great
if you're rich and live in a red state.
Corporate interests save more,
at expense of the poor,
and my own wealth is sure to inflate.[11]

CDC WORD POLICE[12]
DECEMBER 16, 2017

Words like "transgender" and "science-based,"
I dislike so I'll have them erased.
And to strengthen my hand,
the word "fascist" is banned.
With "Dear Leader" I'll have it replaced.

How can I be expected to lead us,
if health agency staff can say "fetus"?
And "diversity" stinks.
Get if off all our links!
We can't permit such words to impede us.

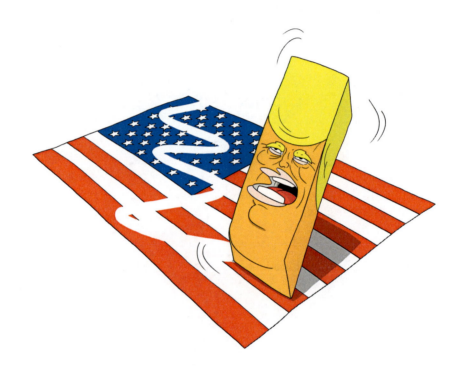

TAX "REFORM"[13]
DECEMBER 21, 2017

Congress gave me a great Christmas gift,
'cause my finances needed a lift.
Guess my populist label
is now well off the table,
though my loyal mob won't get the drift.

We'll keep telling them not to be fickle –
just be patient and wait for the trickle.
It might never arrive,
but investors will thrive.
Would they rather a hammer and sickle?

How to pay for this corporate welfare?
Why not gut programs like Medicare?
This should be no surprise –
just more Trump campaign lies.
Bunk served up by a smug billionaire.

DEEP FREEZE
DECEMBER 29, 2017

With some states in a weekend deep freeze,
global warming's been brought to its knees.
Let's ignore long-term trends.
Climate change theory ends
with the presence of frost on my trees.

Please don't call me a science denier.
In my leadership role I aspire
to a loftier goal:
more crude oil, gas and coal.
Why not let ozone levels go higher?

Those clean energy flakes are a drag.
I'll keep making America gag.
Let the countries who care
save their water and air,
while our grandchildren breathe through a bag.

They say ignorance is like cloud nine.
Empty-headed bliss suits me just fine.
How I finished with college
so unburdened by knowledge
is a mystery hard to untwine.

 Donald J. Trump
@realDonaldTrump

In the East, it could be the COLDEST New Year's Eve on record. Perhaps we could use a little bit of that good old Global Warming that our Country, but not other countries, was going to pay TRILLIONS OF DOLLARS to protect against. Bundle up!

5:01 PM - Dec 28, 2017

HAVE A SAFE FLIGHT
JANUARY 2, 2018

If you ever have wondered just why
planes are able to stay in the sky –
There's a clear correlation:
I'm strict on aviation.
Without me, you would certainly die.

Thanks to me, you can have a safe flight,
and the future's incredibly bright.
The sun burst from a cloud,
and for that I'm so proud.
After all, I invented daylight.

I'm the source of outcomes that are good.
I succeed where nobody else could.
But if things go awry,
then blame some other guy.
Can't be me 'cause I'm bound for sainthood.

Donald J. Trump @realDonaldTrump

Since taking office I have been very strict on Commercial Aviation. Good news - it was just reported that there were Zero deaths in 2017, the best and safest year on record!

6:13 AM - 2 Jan 2018

MY NUKE BUTTON
JANUARY 3, 2018

My nuke button's much bigger than yours.
I just love to massage its contours.
We're a tantrum away
from a mushroom cloud day –
a tweet storm causing nuclear wars.
(Armageddon to even some scores.)
(Build strong bomb shelters under your floors.)
(Radiation can cause nasty sores.)
(I'm the vacuum that nature abhors.)

I'm the sheriff of fierce rhetoric.
I talk loudly and wield a small stick.
I give Kim such a scare,
he keeps filling the air
with test missiles, that arrogant prick![14]

North Korean Leader Kim Jong Un just stated that the "Nuclear Button is on his desk at all times." Will someone from his depleted and food starved regime please inform him that I too have a Nuclear Button, but it is a much bigger & more powerful one than his, and my Button works!

4:49 PM - Jan 2, 2018

DOING GRAMMAR (AND EVERYTHING ELSE) PROPER[15]
JANUARY 6, 2018

This whole Russia inquest is a ruse.
It's so sad that Jeff chose to recuse.
I "do everything proper" –
less a crook than a copper.
Never met an adverb I could use (except "bigly").

STABLE GENIUS
JANUARY 7, 2018

"Stable genius" defines who I am.
I'm a lion and never a lamb.
And I'm "like, really smart,"
raising cons to an art.
All attacks against me are a sham.

> **Donald J. Trump**
> @realDonaldTrump
>
> ....Actually, throughout my life, my two greatest assets have been mental stability and being, like, really smart. Crooked Hillary Clinton also played these cards very hard and, as everyone knows, went down in flames. I went from VERY successful businessman, to top T.V. Star.....

> **Donald J. Trump**
> @realDonaldTrump
>
> ....to President of the United States (on my first try). I think that would qualify as not smart, but genius....and a very stable genius at that!

FIRE AND FURY[16]
JANUARY 7, 2018

Fire and Fury is making me blue.
I've directed my lawyers to sue.
There should be prior restraint
when a clown tries to paint
me as someone who hasn't a clue.

SHITHOLE COUNTRIES[17]
JANUARY 11, 2018

If your people have skin black as coal,
then your country must be a shithole.
But I'd really be fond
if you're Norwegian blond.
All white immigrants will be my goal.

STORMY[18]
JANUARY 19, 2018

Since Melania couldn't endure me,
thought I'd schedule a session with Stormy.
She'd do something obscene
with my *Forbes* magazine.
It's those whacks on the ass that restore me.
(Looking for kinky sex that won't bore me.)
(How could any porn star not adore me?)

GOVERNMENT SHUTDOWN[19]
JANUARY 20, 2018

Budget talks reached a bitter impasse,
'cause I said something racist and crass.
I reneged on a deal.
Now the impact is real.
Shouldn't listen to Miller blow gas.

Mitch would like my position defined.
Graham complains I won't make up my mind.
And I'm hearing a rumor
that the nasty Chuck Schumer
has made statements that aren't too kind.

Help for dreamers I want to forestall,
till there's funding for my stupid wall.
Mexico isn't nice –
they won't cover the price.
So our taxpayers must take the fall.

Eighteen billion's a small price to pay,
though there's hardly a crossing, they say.
It was my campaign pledge.
Could we just plant a hedge?
Would that keep immigration at bay?

I'll just sit back while John Kelly tries
to undo damage done by my lies.
I'll resort to a tweet
while the rest of them meet.
If I lead, then I can't criticize.

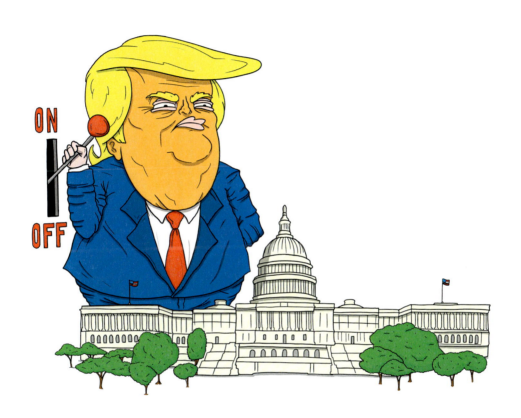

I'VE GOT THOSE INVESTIGATION BLUES[20]
JANUARY 26, 2018

To obstruct never was my intent.
I just wanted the probes to relent.
When I said to McGahn,
"go and fire that man,"
it was merely an effort to vent.

The same goes for the Comey affair.
I just fired him to help clear the air.
And had Jeff showed some spunk,
wouldn't be in this funk –
we'd have no Special Counsel out there.

I want Mueller to interview me,
'cause I'll prove that there's nothing to see.
But if my lawyers say
to keep out of his way,
I'll avoid Mueller's deft third degree.

Meanwhile I'll send my minions to claim
it's a plot to destroy my good name,
yell "corrupt FBI,"
and if that doesn't fly,
there is always Obama to blame.

NUNES MEMO[21]
FEBRUARY 2, 2018

When conditions get tough on the Hill,
what I need is an amoral shill.
There's a fellow named Devin,
who's like manna from heaven.
He can author false memos with skill.

He'll disclose secret methods and sources,
jeopardizing intelligence forces.
But they're small sacrifices
to distract from my vices.
Democrats should get off their high horses.

I want cherry-picked details revealed.
If it's classified, get it unsealed.
Let's be sure that we scuttle
any fact-based rebuttal,
and my tax returns remain concealed.

I appointed that Christopher Wray.
Now he's trying to stand in my way
'cause I'm peddling lies
Why is that a surprise?
It's how I celebrate Groundhog Day.

AMERICAN DISGRACE (AND BAD SPELLER) [22]
FEBRUARY 4, 2018

The FBI's been so unfair.
There corruption is beyond compare.
There hunting for witches
has run into glitches.
This memo proves their's no their their.

Now the "Trump" vindication's complete.
And this victory odor is sweet.
It provides me the nod
to eliminate Rod,
so that Mueller I'm free to unseat.

Donald J. Trump ✓
@realDonaldTrump

This memo totally vindicates "Trump" in probe. But the Russian Witch Hunt goes on and on. Their was no Collusion and there was no Obstruction (the word now used because, after one year of looking endlessly and finding NOTHING, collusion is dead). This is an American disgrace!

6:40 AM · Feb 3, 2018

TREASON[23]
FEBRUARY 5, 2018

I'm disturbed that the nasty black caucus
sat and stared like they want to plank-walk us.
When I self-hype with lies,
they should still cheer and rise.
They were mute when they should have been raucous.

If my actions tend toward the despotic
and my statements all seem idiotic,
your disdain must be checked.
You must show me respect.
If you don't, then you're unpatriotic.

When there's any good news, I'm the reason.
Toward my false claims you'd best be appeasin'.
If I perpetrate fraud,
you must loudly applaud.
When you don't clap, it constitutes treason.

I LOVE A PARADE[24]
FEBRUARY 7, 2018

I would love an armed forces parade.
It will make adversaries afraid.
I will not be outdone
by that thug Kim Jong-Un.
Military might should be displayed.

I'll ascend a review stand and wave.
It's the kind of attention I crave.
They'll give fervent salutes.
And I'd wear some jackboots
if my bone spurs will only behave.

The cost likely will be several mil,
but so worth it to give me a thrill.
I'll make like Mussolini –
boost the size of my weenie,
while the taxpayers shoulder the bill.

BEAT YOUR WIFE, GET A WHITE HOUSE JOB[25]
FEBRUARY 8, 2018

Migrants must receive vetting extreme,
separating the milk from the cream.
But for my inner sanctum,
we've so seldomly ranked 'em.
Fog a mirror? Come serve on my team!

When the FBI warned about Rob,
we just felt he should still have the job.
Severe spousal abuse
shouldn't act as a noose.
Was it wrong to protect Hope's heartthrob?

Couldn't get full security clearance.
Why should that nuance cause interference?
He punched more than one spouse,
so deserves the White House.
Do our standards for hire lack coherence?

Poor Rob Porter, we'll certainly miss you.
For your wives we don't carry a tissue.
You would still be our guy,
but a pictured black eye
turned this into a big PR issue.

WAITING IN THE WINGS[26]
FEBRUARY 10, 2018

I'm real fond of the loyal Mike Pence.
He's my envoy to sporting events.
Always late to the scoop.
Never seems in the loop.
But obsequious in my defense.

He's so willing to carry my bags.
He despises cross-dressers and fags.
He'll depart a big game
to put kneelers to shame,
and won't stand when he sees other flags.

He now patiently waits in the wings
to see what end the Mueller probe brings.
Hopes to slide to my place
if I fall in disgrace.
He'll be there when the fat lady sings.

NO INTELLIGENCE HERE[27]
FEBRUARY 11, 2018

Since I'm such an extremely smart person,
I don't need to read chapter and verse in
those "intelligence briefs."
This Commander-in-Chief's
not in need of key knowledge dispersin'.

To entice me they made it one page.
But it's too dense for me to engage.
So I'll get up to speed
with each day's Fox News feed.
I'm already a world affairs sage.

Don't confuse me with salient facts.
They're the drug of elite wonks and hacks.
I disdain expertise.
Only compliments, please!
I want love from my closest contacts.

PARKLAND, FLORIDA
(VALENTINE'S DAY MASSACRE)[28]
FEBRUARY 14, 2018

We're the fine folks of your NRA,
sending greetings on Valentine's Day.
We love AR-15s
with immense magazines.
It's too bad if kids get in the way.

Real solutions we'll keep on delaying,
instead opting for thinking and praying.
We'll spread plenty of cash
to ensure no backlash,
and keep weak legislators from straying.

MORE PARKLAND, FLORIDA[29]
FEBRUARY 15, 2018

To address this I need a wordsmith
who'll convey that my grief's not a myth.
Can't discuss gun control –
sold the lobby my soul
(if, in fact, I had one to start with).

I'll tell children they're "never alone,"
though it's plain my support's not full-blown.
My true message is clear:
gun nuts need have no fear.
I'm just throwing the victims a bone.

I'll continue to spout platitudes
till we change anti-gun attitudes.
They are just metal tools.
Regulating's for fools.

I hate when cogent thinking intrudes.
I know too many children have died.
It's important they learn how to hide.
And it shouldn't be hard
to hire one more school guard.
Why can't these great solutions be tried?
In the face of each new shooting spree,
your munitions remain safe with me.
Though events are traumatic,
keep your Colt automatic.
NRA pays my protection fee.

MORE INDICTMENT EXCITEMENT[30]
FEBRUARY 18, 2018

So the Russians sent me a troll farm.
Doesn't mean that they caused any harm.
Clinton animus sown,
but I won on my own,
with my good looks, charisma and charm.

To ensure that democracy fails,
my friend Vlad placed his foot on the scales.
He was lending his weight
to make 'Merica great,
and just adding some wind to my sails.

Mueller said that our role was unwitting,
which for my entourage would be fitting.
But if he tracks my money,
the outcome won't be funny.
There's no jury that would be acquitting.

This indictment's exploding my head,
since they're saying it's only one thread.
Doesn't deal with the hacks
or obstructive attacks.
Add them up and my tenure is dead.

PARKLAND, FLORIDA REVISITED
(OR THE ONLY THING THAT CAN STOP A BAD GUY WITH AN AR-15 AND HIGH-CAPACITY MAGAZINE IS A TEACHER WITH A HANDGUN AND A SMALL BONUS)[31]
FEBRUARY 22, 2018

I want teachers to tote while they teach
and church pastors to pack while they preach.
My ideas are the best.
Let's restore the Wild West
and throw more weapons into the breach.

A mall clothing store clerk or cashier
should conceal a Glock in her brassiere.
It all makes perfect sense:
we can quickly dispense
justice like we did on the frontier.

We'll still let you buy weapons of war
that can wipe people out by the score.
And since some are real fiends
for those large magazines,
we won't talk about them anymore.

These solutions are so very wise.
They ensure that I don't jeopardize
my immense revenue
from the NRA crew,
as they'll see gun and ammo sales rise.

I'll tell shooting survivors I hear them,
while my surrogates work hard to smear them.
Those kids cause me to squirm.
They could sway the mid-term,
which is more than good reason to fear them.

PENNSYLVANIA GERRYMANDERING
FEBRUARY 25, 2018

It's unfair to correct the unfair.
Our courts can't be allowed to go there.
If it hurts GOP,
then we can't let it be!
We have so few House members to spare.

Who's this Gerry and how did he mander?
Did he cause district lines to meander?
Did he help rig the vote,
floating my party's boat?
Did that stir up the Democrats' dander?

Let's ignore both the law and the facts.
The sole question is who it impacts.
We can change boundaries
any way that we please,
just so long as Dem votes it subtracts.

Democrat judges have totally redrawn election lines in the great State of Pennsylvania. @FoxNews. This is very unfair to Republicans and to our country as a whole. Must be appealed to the United States Supreme Court ASAP!

12:16 PM - Feb 24, 2018

PARKLAND, FLORIDA AGAIN[32]
FEBRUARY 27, 2018

I'd go running right into that school.
I'm so brave and so strong and so cool.
Now that bone spurs have healed,
I am ready to wield
super-hero traits in any duel.

Well-armed thugs must obey my commands
or be throttled with my tiny hands.
I'm your kid's best defense
and with Deputy Pence,
I'll be sheriff of these here badlands.

I will serve as your child's human shield.
With my bulk, the threshold will be sealed.
I'll jump into the fray
and the bad guys will pay.
I'm a force on the school battlefield.

I don't need any kind of a gun.
I'll just wrestle the perp one-on-one.
If you think this is true,
I've a bridge to sell you.
Sharing these fantasies is such fun.

LOSING HOPE[33]
FEBRUARY 28, 2018

Her decision took me by surprise.
Guess she's tired of telling white lies.
Now she's sprouting her wings,
and I'll say, as Hope springs,
that eternal fealty would be wise.

She'll be called for a tough interview
by Bob Mueller and his nasty crew.
I'll be on high alert,
'cause there's plenty of dirt
she could spread if she really wants to.

Hope and I once were joined at the hip,
but she now is abandoning ship.
This thing has me on edge.
Need a loyalty pledge!
Will the Mueller team get her to flip?

You could say that I'm now losing Hope.
I don't know how I'm going to cope.
I'm beginning to smart
as my minions depart
and the Russia probe broadens in scope.

SESSIONS![34]
MARCH 1, 2018

I'm upset with that Mr. Magoo.
He won't do what I want him to do.
I should just do away
with the whole DOJ,
so they cannot uncover what's true.

TARIFFS[35]
MARCH 1, 2018

I'm declaring a global trade war.
All those experts I chose to ignore.
Watch the stock prices fall.
Higher costs for us all.
Economic recession in store.

Being obstinate gives satisfaction,
plus I need to create a distraction.
It's not such a big deal.
We'll have more home-made steel
while they tariff our goods in reaction.

Well, so much for your measly tax break.
You'll pay lots more for products we make.
And our exports will dive
as once-allies contrive
to get vengeance for my huge mistake.

LYING[36]
MARCH 2, 2018

I distort, fabricate and embellish,
lie, mislead and dissemble with relish.
It will make your mind boggle,
how I blithely hornswoggle.
Tracking all my untruths can be hellish.

I will perjure, deceive and delude.
Can't unscramble the nonsense I've spewed.
I'll tap dance with the truth
and be really uncouth.
I embody moral turpitude.

I will falsify who, what, where, when,
and slip in a tall tale now and then.
All this lying's such fun
that as soon as I'm done,
I'll just start in all over again.

BEN CARSON'S FURNITURE[37]
MARCH 3, 2018

Let's cut funds for the poor and disabled,
so that Ben can be regally tabled.
Like Mnuchin and Pruitt,
without thought he'll just do it.
Chutzpah's how this is properly labeled.

NUNBERG[38]
MARCH 6, 2018

As more proof that I employ the best,
I would place Sam Nunberg at the crest.
Against all good advice,
went and hired him twice.
Now you've heard him and aren't you impressed?

Wants to tell the Grand Jury, "Forget it."
In a very short time he'll regret it.
Won't turn over email?
That would land him in jail.
If you think he'll hold out, wouldn't bet it.

Serving jail time, he won't be alone.
He'll have Mike, Paul and old Roger Stone.[39]
And right in the next cell,
there'll be Jared as well,
calling Qatar to cover his loan.[40]

While this whack job ex-aide of mine rambles,
my executive branch is in shambles,
because working for me
is a hazard, you see,
and no sane person takes on such gambles.[41]

COHN RESIGNATION[42]
MARCH 6, 2018

Now I've lost "globalist" Gary Cohn.
Pretty soon I'll be here all alone.
I'm surrounded by gloom.
No adults in the room.
This White House is a talent-free zone.

CHAOS AND TURNOVER[43]
MARCH 6, 2018

With my aides I like conflict and fighting,
disagreements, crossed swords and backbiting.
The main reason I hire them
is that then I can fire them.
This reality show's so exciting!

People leave at a pace that's frenetic --
a propensity so "energetic."
I encourage their views,
but dissent is "fake news."
If you doubt me, then you are pathetic.

I have nothing but love and affection
for each argument, leak and defection.
When chaos is the norm,
it's a daily shit-storm.
Now that's what I would call pure "perfection."

In the end, I take my own advice.
My keen mind is an awesome device.
Using impulse and whim,
I'll go out on a limb.
I inhabit a fool's paradise.

The new Fake News narrative is that there is CHAOS in the White House. Wrong! People will always come & go, and I want strong dialogue before making a final decision. I still have some people that I want to change (always seeking perfection). There is no Chaos, only great Energy!

4:55 AM - Mar 6, 2018

BACK PEDDLING ON GUN CONTROL[44]
MARCH 13, 2018

I told Senator Toomey, "Be brave.
There are so many children to save.
You should not own a gun
until age twenty-one."
But the NRA knew I would cave.

I would never set up a commission
(unless serving the gun lobby's mission).
I put on a good show,
but if Wayne tells me so,
I'll arm teachers with nuclear fission.

FED UP WITH REX[45]
MARCH 13, 2018

I just ended my long-running spat
with the guy who was chief diplomat.
I have now closed the door on
that poor fool who said "moron,"
as my ship loses yet one more rat.

I decided to dump him by tweet.
It's so quick and so firm and so neat.
But I thanked him so much.
That's my personal touch,
when I'd rather not bother to meet.

While the press dwells on porn star affairs,
I keep moving Titanic deck chairs.
As old Rex takes a hike,
I'll send Gina and Mike
to inhabit this dark den of bears.

With Pompeo's Department of State,
I'll continue to alienate
all our allies and friends
on whom peacetime depends.
Isolation will make us so great!

MORE ON (MORON) REX
MARCH 13, 2018

I'm announcing my purge of the week.
On this team, I will brook no more cheek.
Take your loyalty oath,
cut off one ball or both,
and I'll have all the "yes men" I seek.

I've sent Tillerson into Rexile.
His departure is making me smile.
His Rexpulsion complete,
he'll Rexit to the street.
Don't Rexpect to see him for awhile.

STAFF PARANOIA[46]
MARCH 16, 2018

I want aides to remain on their toes.
It's much better if nobody knows
if they're here or they're gone.
At the mercy of Don!
Watching which way my fickle wind blows.

I like people to feel on the edge.
I'm excited when driving a wedge.
From one minute to next,
they'll be bothered and vexed,
wond'ring when they'll be shoved off a ledge.

Hearing rumors H.R. won't be spared,
our whole personnel unit got scared.
They expected disaster,
but then learned it's McMaster
and their jobs are (for now) unimpaired.

All my staffers should be paranoid –
concerned whether I'm glad or annoyed.
Like each Donald Trump wife:
Do they have a shelf life?
And how long till their lives are destroyed?

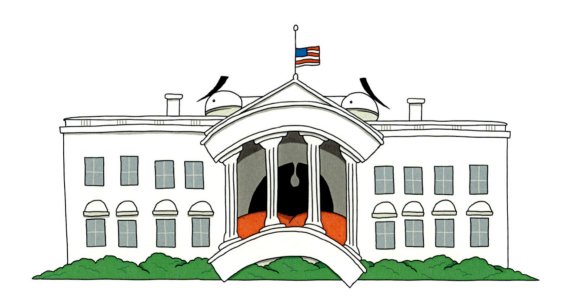

MORE MUELLER TIME[47]
MARCH 20, 2018

I'm indebted to tough oligarchs.
The Trump family were such easy marks.
Though I used to say thanks
to those nice Russian banks,
now the Mueller team's circling like sharks.

THUNDERCLOUDS ON THE HORIZON[48]
MARCH 20, 2018

I'm not sure I can weather this storm.
It was hard to resist her fine form.
I just couldn't abstain
from this blonde hurricane.
Now it's causing a media swarm.

I dispatched my long-time fixer goon
to buy silence from this wild typhoon.
She accepted the cash.
Now she's making a splash,
while I'm playing the sex-crazed buffoon.

PUTIN ON THE RITZ[49]
MARCH 21, 2018

I called Putin to say, "Mazel Tov!"
Always praise him when push comes to shove.
Can't display enmity
when he has goods on me.
So I need to keep showing him love.

TARIFFS ON CHINA[50]
MARCH 22, 2018

I'm a literal China shop bull.
Start trade wars with the crap that I pull.
Never act with due care.
Now the market's a bear
'cause the space 'tween my ears is just wool.

BYE BYE H.R.[51]
MARCH 23, 2018

Though McMaster was just down the hall,
I extinguished him in a phone call.
Sarah said yesterday
he and I were okay.
Must have shocked him to see the ax fall.

I've appointed the hawkish John Bolton,
though, to me, his mustache is revoltin'.
Has a bellicose knack.
Pushed for war in Iraq.
Proof my gray matter's getting more molten.

IMMIGRANT CARAVANS[52]
APRIL 1, 2018

I don't care about DACA at all.
Just a bargaining chip for my wall.
Those kids might have their dreams,
but they're grist for my schemes
to ensure that the Dems take a fall.

It's a program Obama created,
which I think is good reason to hate it.
So I had it thrown out,
tried to use it for clout,
but no deal ever was consummated.

I'll claim immigrant caravans flow,
saying DACA's the reason they go.
These assertions are lies,
since no one qualifies
who arrived less than 12 years ago.

Donald J. Trump
@realDonaldTrump

Border Patrol Agents are not allowed to properly do their job at the Border because of ridiculous liberal (Democrat) laws like Catch & Release. Getting more dangerous. "Caravans" coming. Republicans must go to Nuclear Option to pass tough laws NOW. NO MORE DACA DEAL!

6:56 AM - Apr 1, 2018

> Mexico is doing very little, if not NOTHING, at stopping people from flowing into Mexico through their Southern Border, and then into the U.S. They laugh at our dumb immigration laws. They must stop the big drug and people flows, or I will stop their cash cow, NAFTA. NEED WALL!
>
> 7:25 AM - Apr 1, 2018

> These big flows of people are all trying to take advantage of DACA. They want in on the act!
>
> 7:28 AM - Apr 1, 2018

ANOTHER BUSY WEEK
APRIL 3, 2018

I enjoy news produced by Sinclair.[53]
All the other outlets are unfair.
Since they're singing my tune,
they can merge with Tribune.
Then I'll have propaganda to spare.

I despise that Jeff Bezos[54] the most,
'cause he owns the fake *Washington Post*.
And he heads Amazon:
Brick and mortars are gone,
which is turning my business to toast!

It's so easy to win a trade war,
till the other guy evens the score.
Now we can't sell our pork
and I feel like a dork,
as they hit us with tariffs galore.[55]
(Were things better with China before?)

PRUITT BLEW IT[56]
APRIL 6, 2018

Why are critics attacking Scott Pruitt?
When I want air polluted, he'll do it.
He has excellent taste
in industrial waste,
and allows its producers to spew it.
(He prefers that a river runs through it.)

Pays low rent to a lobbyist's wife.
Orders sirens to ease traffic strife.
Has a wonderful time
on the taxpayers' dime.
With corruption this man's pretty rife.

But he's done everything I desired.
By those oil and coal groups he's admired.
If permitted to stay,
he'll destroy EPA.
So I don't want to tell him he's fired.

And by keeping him on, I'll be free
to sack Jeff and make Scott my AG.
Then, with my complete backing,
he'll send Bob Mueller packing.
That's a prospect I'd welcome with glee.
(Let's make real this sublime fantasy!)

IT'S MY LAWYER'S FAULT![57]
APRIL 6, 2018

Didn't know that her silence he'd fund.
When I learned that he did, I was stunned!
I knew nothing at all.
Cohen must take the fall.
I don't like that we're getting outgunned.

Guess this means we have no binding deal
and that Stormy is now free to squeal.
We tried buying her off.
Her response was to scoff.
My transgressions are tough to conceal.

BLAZING TOWER[58]
APRIL 7, 2018

In my tower fire somebody died.
I responded by gushing with pride.
Forget resident screams.
We had well-built steel beams!
Why waste money on sprinklers inside?

>
>
> Fire at Trump Tower is out. Very confined (well built building). Firemen (and women) did a great job. THANK YOU!
>
> 3:42 PM - Apr 7, 2018

THEY RAIDED MY LAWYER[59]
APRIL 10, 2018

For a no-knock search warrant on Cohen,
They would need an extremely strong showin'.
But since this is my lawyer,
they should stay in the foyer,
while he gets a destructive blaze blowin'.

What's this nonsense about "rule of law"?
It's beginning to stick in my craw.
Bank fraud, threats, dirty deals?
I do those between meals!
Business methods I'd never withdraw.

This cruel search was an unlawful break-in.
If they say there's due process they're fakin'.
It's a conspiracy
to hang something on me,
and disloyal RINOs are partakin'!

COMEY AND SCOOTER[60]
APRIL 13, 2018

I'll call Comey a leaker and liar,
who it was my great honor to fire.
Him we should prosecute,
but I'll pardon the Scoot,
so my loyal sidekicks won't perspire.

Manafort, Michael Flynn and Rick Gates
needn't fear that disaster awaits.
If they don't rat on me,
I'll ensure they're set free.
I'm the guy who determines their fates.

But Mike Cohen is more problematic,
with those files and tapes up in his attic.
Things could turn pretty sordid
if my crimes were recorded,
even though my denials are emphatic.

Donald J. Trump
@realDonaldTrump

James Comey is a proven LEAKER & LIAR. Virtually everyone in Washington thought he should be fired for the terrible job he did–until he was, in fact, fired. He leaked CLASSIFIED information, for which he should be prosecuted. He lied to Congress under OATH. He is a weak and.....

5:01 AM - Apr 13, 2018

> **Donald J. Trump**
> @realDonaldTrump
>
> ....untruthful slime ball who was, as time has proven, a terrible Director of the FBI. His handling of the Crooked Hillary Clinton case, and the events surrounding it, will go down as one of the worst "botch jobs" of history. It was my great honor to fire James Comey!
>
> 5:17 AM - Apr 13, 2018

RUDY FRUITY[51]
MAY 5, 2018

The sheer number of times that I've lied
is so large, it can't be quantified.
And with bozos like Rudy
hired to cover my booty,
all the sleaze becomes harder to hide.

When you pay to have escapades hushed
and your dirty transgressions air-brushed,
mask your financing trail.
Your concealment will fail
if the funds aren't sufficiently slushed.

ZTE AND ME[62]
MAY 14, 2018

I send thanks to my friend Xi Jinping.
Half a billion's a beautiful thing.
We'll assist ZTE,
'cause there's something for me.
It's a deal I was happy to swing.

We should help put more Chinese to work,
if it brings me a personal perk.
My priorities switched
when my purse was enriched.
My corruption's much more than a quirk.

I want Beijing's folks fully employed.
When that happens, my spirits are buoyed.
Am I mad, high on blow?
It's about quid pro quo!
There's no need to consult Sigmund Freud.

Chinese business should be fully staffed.
Am I sounding deluded or daft?
Foreign aid gets increased
when they keep my palms greased.
My best talent's engaging in graft.

MISSING THE GOOD OLE DAYS[63]
MAY 20, 2018

Firing people on my TV show.
Bilking contractors out of their dough.
Doing white collar crimes.
Those were wonderful times!
How I'm longing to bask in their glow.

Fake news outlets don't show me respect.
Robert Mueller thinks I'm a suspect.
All my bluster and bluff
somehow isn't enough.
This is hard for my low intellect.

I had mastered the art of the deal.
Now there's hardly a one I can seal.
And those partisan spies
keep exposing my lies.
They don't care how mistreated I feel.

Fights with Iran, Korea and China
are beginning to give me angina.
My life's filled with such stress.
It was calm and far less
complicated in Stormy's vagina.

SUMMIT FEVER[64]
MAY 24, 2018

Kim Jong-Un: What a nasty Korean!
He's my least favorite human bein'.
Self-aggrandizing brat
and tyrannical rat.
Is that my own reflection I'm seein'?

I thought his behavior was crummy
when Rocket Man called Pence a dummy.
Never call people names.
That will just fan the flames.
It's much smarter to act like you're chummy.

I so wanted that nuclear summit.
Souvenir gold coins could be sold from it.
I should break Bolton's tibia –
Why did he mention Libya?
It caused chances for détente to plummet.

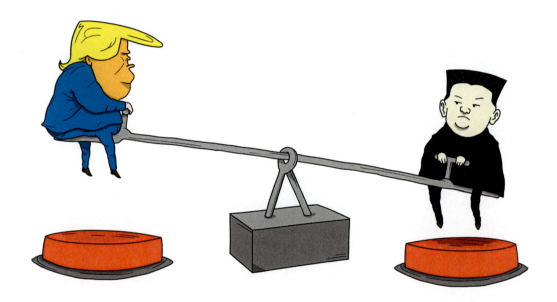

JACK JOHNSON[55]
MAY 24, 2018

No one else thought of pardoning Jack.
This proves I'm your best friend if you're black.
I have learned how to pander,
and my gestures are grander
than your average political hack.

Then, again, there's the Central Park Five.
And my Obama birth papers jive.
And my lengthy delay
to denounce KKK.
I've worked hard to help racism thrive.

Our black citizens might be oppressed,
but pro athletes should give it a rest.
So I surely won't mind
if they're skewered and fined
for engaging in peaceful protest.

A TRUMPIAN COMMENCEMENT SPEECH[66]
MAY 25, 2018

Until me, no one gave you a raise.
So I come here expecting your praise.
With one word from my lips,
you'll have hundreds more ships.
I demand your affection displays.

As a tribute to your graduation,
I'll engage in self-congratulation.
Blatant lies I'll disperse
from my alt-universe,
as I seek underserved adulation.

I'll impart these life lessons and tools:
Truthful discourse is for chumps and fools.
Your most fervent devotion
should be crass self-promotion,
and avoiding adherence to rules.

You'll learn integrity is for naught.
Let the world know that you can be bought.
Careful study's a waste.
Make decisions in haste.
Expert input should rarely be sought.

As our next generation of leaders,
do not squander your time being readers.
Use corruption and stealth
to accumulate wealth,
and associate with bottom feeders.

Never search for a kinder solution.
Leave your children with loads of pollution.
It's okay to defame
and to always shift blame.
Denigrate each revered institution.

Treat the judicial branch with contempt.
Hold yourself out as conflicts exempt.
Citizens want to learn
what's in your tax return?
Firmly shut down their every attempt.

Run up mountains of national debt,
if it buys your rich friends a new jet.
Instill fear and race hate.
Claim that's making us great.
Accept all of the graft you can get.

Say that most neo-Nazis are good.
Then complain you were misunderstood.
If the press calls you out,
allege bias, then pout.
Use the mantle of false victimhood.

PUTTING THE "ME" IN MEMORIAL DAY
MAY 28, 2018

On this solemn Memorial Day,
I have words of importance to say.
I believe you'll agree
that it's all about me.
This should melt all your sorrow away.

Your loved one paid the ultimate price,
but I know that he wouldn't think twice,
'cause with me at the helm,
all is well in the realm.
I'm declaring this holiday "Nice!"

Donald J. Trump ✓
@realDonaldTrump

Happy Memorial Day! Those who died for our great country would be very happy and proud at how well our country is doing today. Best economy in decades, lowest unemployment numbers for Blacks and Hispanics EVER (& women in 18years), rebuilding our Military and so much more. Nice!

5:58 AM - May 28, 2018

ROSEANNE GETS BARRED[67]
MAY 30, 2018

My poor near-sighted friend named Roseanne
can't distinguish an ape from a man.
Never took science classes
and needs much stronger glasses.
She's been doing the best that she can.

That they canceled her show is a shame.
She should not have been saddled with blame.
Just a brief aberration,
caused by sleep medication,
has destroyed this fine woman's good name.

She's an avid conspiracy buff.
Her career just went up in a puff.
But there's no need for moans –
She can join Alex Jones,
selling more false and outrageous stuff.

You won't find me condemning her tweet,
'cause I think that her comments were neat.
What's a bigoted joke
among privileged white folk?
Plus she cured it by pressing "delete."
(And, to my base, this stuff is red meat.)

I'll employ this occasion to whine:
Is this where ABC draws the line?
Inconsistent Bob Iger
executed this tiger.
Can't he make news on me more benign?

> **Donald J. Trump**
> @realDonaldTrump
>
> Bob Iger of ABC called Valerie Jarrett to let her know that "ABC does not tolerate comments like those" made by Roseanne Barr. Gee, he never called President Donald J. Trump to apologize for the HORRIBLE statements made and said about me on ABC. Maybe I just didn't get the call?
>
> 8:31 AM - May 30, 2018

SPYGATE[68]
MAY 31, 2018

This whole Russia witch hunt has me irate,
so I'll make up a drama called "Spygate".
Whether proven or not,
it's an anti-Trump plot!
(Says the world's most delusional primate.)

I don't need any basis in fact.
It's sufficient that this will distract.
My defensive playbook:
Claim the cop is a crook.
Watch the uninformed over-react.

But it didn't work out as I planned.
On this one I was clearly outmanned.
Trey said, "Nothing to see."
Even Fox betrayed me!
No one followed me to fairyland!

CARNAC[69]
JUNE 2, 2018

Did I open Kim's letter or not?
In an eight minute span I forgot.
Since clairvoyance I lack
and I'm sure no Carnac,
guess I'll read it to find out the plot.

I just know that the content was nice.
Once I see it I'll be more precise.
But it's so hard to cope
with that huge envelope!
Someone brief me and offer advice.

PARDON ME![70]
JUNE 4, 2018

Mueller's inquest is making me moody,
so I need an attack dog like Rudy.
Says the stupidest things,
but I hope that he flings
a game-saving Hail Mary like Flutie.

I denied writing Don Junior's letter,
but my lawyers remember it better.
Can't keep our stories straight.
Should we call it "Liegate"?
Build my brand as mendacious trendsetter?

As the truth I continue to fudge,
I've declared I can be my own judge.
Once the charges have hardened,
I'll say, "Donald, you're pardoned!"
Such compassion I'd never begrudge.

 Donald J. Trump
@realDonaldTrump

As has been stated by numerous legal scholars, I have the absolute right to PARDON myself, but why would I do that when I have done nothing wrong? In the meantime, the never ending Witch Hunt, led by 13 very Angry and Conflicted Democrats (& others) continues into the mid-terms!

5:35 AM - Jun 4, 2018

GOD BLESS AMERICA![71]
JUNE 5, 2018

"God Bless 'Merica" isn't real long.
Someone teach me the words to that song.
Tried to be patriotic,
but I looked idiotic.
My lip-syncing went terribly wrong.

Something something then land that I love.
Dee dee dee dee da da da above.
Dum dee dum came a spider.
La la la la beside her.
Prairies, mountains, a fish and a dove?

SEPARATING FAMILIES[72]
JUNE 5, 2018

Let's treat migrants like beasts from the wild.
Separate each young mom from her child.
Is it morally right?
Hell, their skin isn't white!
I can't let our homeland be defiled.

As I rip babes away from their mothers,
I'll send tweets that attempt to blame others.
The directive's my own,
but the Dems should atone.
I'd adopt these kids, given my druthers.

Donald J. Trump
@realDonaldTrump

Separating families at the Border is the fault of bad legislation passed by the Democrats. Border Security laws should be changed but the Dems can't get their act together! Started the Wall.

4:58 AM - Jun 5, 2018

WATER BOTTLE PROTOCOL[73]
JUNE 6, 2018

Mikey Pence is my top sycophant.
I show him what he can do and can't.
He knows deference matters;
earnest mimicry flatters.
Plus his own personality's scant.

DIPPY DIPLOMACY/DUMB-IT SUMMIT[74]
JUNE 7, 2018

I've invented a new platitude –
that it's all about tough attitude.
There's no need to prepare.
I'll just blow some hot air.
Ignorance leaves me great latitude.

G-7 SUMMIT
JUNE 9, 2018

In my quest to make Putin my pal, I
keep on alienating each ally.
Merkel, Trudeau and May
try to hold me at bay,
while Macron wants to give me the mal eye.

I'm the world's most adept diplomat.
I engage every friend in a spat.
Isolation is fun.
It's G-8 or G-none!
Multilateral pacts are old hat.

Every time I show up for a meeting,
our prestige in the world takes a beating.
Arrived late and left early.
My behavior was squirrelly.
Reached a deal before rudely retreating.

SINGAPORE FLING[76]
JUNE 12, 2018

I was meeting with Kim one-on-one,
'cause there's selling I want to get done.
Some Trump steaks to export.
A Pyongyang golf resort.
And the leaks from our chat will be none.

Detailed info? There won't be a font.
I can spin this however I want.
It's the handshake that counts.
It'll give me a bounce.
Elbow grasping's as good as détente

Rocket Man doesn't know he's a prop
for my biggest and best photo op.
I'll be hangin' with Kim
but the chances are slim
that this nuclear arms race will stop.

Kim, it's clear that we've bonded like glue.
And I'm sure to your word you'll be true.
I'm a guy you can trust in.
Just ask Shinzo and Justin
and those wonderful folks in EU.

Kim Jong-Un is a "talented man."
Got commitments but offered no plan.
Gained legitimization.
Gave no verification.
It's a lousier deal than Iran!

Joint maneuvers are far too much fuss.
Let's throw SK right under the bus.
A surprising concession?
In my hasty prep session,
it's a small point I failed to discuss.

As I take my smug victory lap,
will I prove to be just one more sap?
Predecessors were proud of
deals NK then backed out of.
Am I falling into the same trap?

MORE LOVE IN SINGAPORE[77]
JUNE 13, 2018

There's no longer a nuclear threat.
So no need to break into a sweat.
Nothing substantive's changed,
but I've tamed the deranged.
Now on Rocket Man's word I would bet.

Kim was friendly, engaging and charming,
and he told me he'd "work toward" disarming.
Then we shook hands and posed.
There's no chance I'll get hosed.
His huge arsenal isn't alarming.

Kim is such a strong principled guy,
that he never would tell me a lie.
Now I think he's a god.
We're like peas in a pod.
He's turned into my staunchest ally.

 Donald J. Trump
@realDonaldTrump

Just landed - a long trip, but everybody can now feel much safer than the day I took office. There is no longer a Nuclear Threat from North Korea. Meeting with Kim Jong Un was an interesting and very positive experience. North Korea has great potential for the future!

2:56 AM - Jun 13, 2018

EXONERATION (NOT)![78]
JUNE 18, 2018

The report is out from the IG,
and it fully exonerates me!
Doesn't deal with collusion.
So this ends all confusion.
How airtight could my innocence be?

Those two guys Horowitz and Chris Wray
know I strongly detest when they say
this report doesn't stain
Mueller's evidence chain,
as I keep moving toward judgment day.

INFESTATION[79]
JUNE 19, 2018

Immigrants are a mass infestation.
Like insects, we should stop their gestation.
We'll create a deterrence:
tear the kids from their parents;
claim the Bible as justification.

God decreed we put kids in a cage,
says Jeff Sessions, that biblical sage.
So I'll use them as barter –
till my wall gets its charter,
I'll continue this moral outrage.

I'll give children severe mental trauma,
as they can't see their dada or mama.
I'll use shameful devices
to put families in crisis,
and then blame the whole mess on Obama.

Donald J. Trump
@realDonaldTrump

Democrats are the problem. They don't care about crime and want illegal immigrants, no matter how bad they may be, to pour into and infest our Country, like MS-13. They can't win on their terrible policies, so they view them as potential voters!

6:52 AM - Jun 19, 2018

FOX NEWS PEANUT GALLERY[80]
JUNE 19, 2018

Annie Coulter says crying's an act,
'cause real toddlers would show greater tact.
Take their parents away?
They'll just shrug, say "okay."
They won't care that their life's been hijacked.

Ingraham says it's no worse than day care.
And what child wouldn't want to go there?
When I'm ready to leave,
will my mom come retrieve?
Will I still have her warm hugs to share?

Then there's always compassionate Corey,
who reacts to the terrible story
of a young child with Downs
with some cruel mocking sounds.
Alt-right pundits in all of their glory!

REVERSAL[81]
JUNE 20, 2018

Looks like my hostage gambit backfired.
Now in recrimination I'm mired.
I'd claimed my policy
couldn't be fixed by me,
but the lease on that sham has expired.

It's okay to give children a scar,
but I really can't stand bad PR.
Guess it didn't "look" nice
that these kids paid a price.
That's just life in this White House clown car.

MELANIA'S JACKET[82]
(WITH APOLOGIES TO DR. SEUSS)
JUNE 21, 2018

Went to Texas to show that I care,
with a jacket that said, "I don't care."
When I wear what I wear,
do I care or not care?
Why are you giving me a blank stare?
(Well, I clearly don't care what I wear!)
(Try interpreting this if you dare.)
(Is there meaning we need to lay bare?)

I told each of the children, "God bless,"
but my clothes said I couldn't care less.
Since I like to give voice,
through sartorial choice,
my intentions are anyone's guess.

Don and me – what a wonderful pair.
Thoughtless gaffes are the standard, not rare.
If you track bad optics,
This is in our top six.
Should we call it the "Wear Care Affair"?

BANNING MUSLIMS[83]
JUNE 27, 2018

My third Muslim ban's been kept alive,
by the stalwart conservative five.
It's the weak "PC" version,
but prohibits excursion
to our land from some Islamic dive.

The court found my ban motives were chaste,
as if speeches and tweets were erased.
They could only rule for me
if they chose to ignore me,
and conclude it's security-based.

I'm aware that this court vote was tight.
Those lib judges went down with a fight.
Mitch saved Gorsuch for me
or who knows where we'd be!
I can now push the Court further right!

Between this and my great southern wall,
swarthy vermin won't muster the gall
to "infest" our fair land.
I am taking a stand
so our culture won't suffer free-fall.

I don't care if they're fleeing oppression.
In my small mind that makes no impression.
If they yearn to breathe free,
it means nothing to me.
Keeping borders closed – that's my obsession.

Why is fouling our shores so essential,
if your home has a "shithole" credential?
I don't want their wet backs in.
Give me pure Anglo-Saxon!
If you're non-white, you're inconsequential.

DON'T SPARE THE ROD (OR MUELLER)[84]
JUNE 28, 2018

Representatives Jordan and Gowdy,
at congressional hearings got rowdy.
Jim unleashed a tirade,
but Rod wasn't afraid.
And Trey's memory seems to be cloudy.

Trey told Rod, in language somewhat strong,
that a year of Bob Mueller's too long.
Though Trey's yelling "no mas," he
took two years with Benghazi
and got virtually everything wrong.

It took Whitewater seven plus years.
All the while there were GOP cheers.
Watergate? Over four.
Iran-Contra? Much more.
And the Cisneros probe has no peers.

Mueller's progress has been sure and steady:
over 20 indictments already.
And when Mike Cohen flips,
it will sink some large ships,
and the Dems will be throwing confetti.

That's why I want this inquest shut down.
Mueller needs to be run out of town.
If it brings him discredit,
I will aid and abet it,
to bring smiles where I now have a frown.

PRUITT DEPARTS (IN STEERAGE)[85]
JULY 5, 2018

I just said fond farewell to Scott Pruitt.
Ethics scandal? He couldn't eschew it.
A corrupt high achiever,
he contracted swamp fever,
and it seems I'm the last one who knew it.

Safe environment wasn't for Pruitt.
Liked our air so thick that you could chew it.
Having no predilection
for the concept "protection,"
to the needs of the earth he said, "Screw it!"

Scott was good but, so sadly, he blew it.
Now I need someone else who will do it:
Decimate in a wink
what we eat, breathe and drink;
take my framework and blindly pursue it.

TAN BAN[86]
JULY 9, 2018

China did this to me out of spite,
and achieved dominance in our fight.
For trade sanctions adverse,
there could be nothing worse,
since my orange became the new white.

MANCHURIAN CANDIDATE (AND PRESIDENT)[87]
JULY 11, 2018

As a willing Manchurian pawn,
to this Kremlin alliance I'm drawn.
Disengage from our friends
to achieve Putin's ends.
Over Vlad I'll continue to fawn.

I get money from Russkie accounts,
but you'll never find out the amounts.
My returns remain hidden –
your inspection unbidden.
Without Russia, all my checks would bounce.

So they helped push the voting my way.
It just means I have more debts to pay.
In our upcoming summit,
Vlad expects a lot from it
and our love will be on full display.

To ensure two-way value aplenty,
he'll again help in '18 and '20.
It's one helluva deal
and to see its appeal,
you don't need to be a cognoscenti.

Meanwhile, I'll keep denying connection
between Russia and winning election.
Let intel "experts" crow.
What do those losers know?
I am playing this game to perfection!

STRZOK, MUELLER, MAY, THE QUEEN, AND PUTIN[88]
JULY 15, 2018

I wish someone would insert a sock
in the mouth of that snide Peter Strzok.
The smug son of a bitch is
showing "hunting for witches"
to be one more rhetorical crock.

Now Bob Mueller indicts several more.
Is he trying to run up the score?
He's found Russian intrusion
with some hints of collusion,
and I'm worried about his encore.

So it's off to Great Britain I go.
Just a brief stop before my big show.
PM May I'll demean,
step in front of the Queen,
and then label the EU our foe.

When I meet with Vlad mano-a-mano,
how will I avoid stepping in guano?
Will our chat in Helsinki
produce something so stinky,
I should go to the summit as "John Doe"?
(Should we dub it the "Spy Versus Con Show"?)

He's the one man I won't criticize.
I'm entranced by his steely blue eyes.
And I'll have no regrets
if he covers my debts,
plus provides a nice hotel franchise.

SO MANY NAMES![89]
JULY 15, 2018

Is it England, Great Britain, U.K.?
I'm confused over it to this day.
Though the names for it vary,
one has John Calipari
while the others have Theresa May.

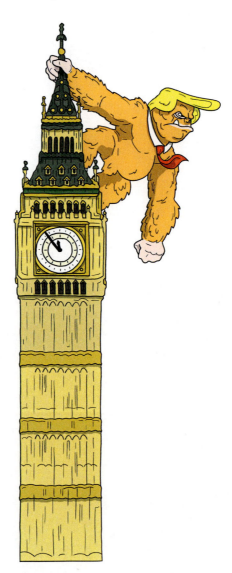

I don't like that one calls itself "great,"
Since, compared to us, they're a lightweight.
And they've stolen my term.
They should be made to squirm.
So I'll sue and then we'll arbitrate.

As for England, I'd never have guessed
that America they once possessed.
Some opponents named George?
A joint called Valley Forge?
And some taxes unwisely assessed?

Since these facts I just recently learned,
It's high time that those English get burned.
Why should we call them friends?
This is where it all ends!
Their attempts at accord will be spurned!
(Here in Trump-land, we'll see the worm turned.)

NO MINYAN IN FINLAND
(SUMMIT FOR PUTIN, NADIR FOR UNITED STATES)[90]
July 16, 2018

When our country gets cyber-attacked,
all that matters is which horse they backed.
We know who, why and how.
So I'm fond of Moscow
for ensuring elections were hacked.

I'm convinced that we all can agree,
when it comes down to letters of three:
CIA I don't trust.
FBI is a bust.
But I love those folks at KGB.

Do you think it will be seen as bad
if I rename D.C. "Putingrad"?
He is such a swell guy,
and that's good reason why
from now on, I'll be calling him dad.

COLLUSION? NOT AN ILLUSION![91]
JULY 17, 2018

He's a dictator cruel and abusive,
but my praise of him's always effusive.
Placed his foot on the scale
to make Hillary fail.
Who could doubt that this plan was collusive?

Would they interfere? I don't know why.
Couldn't dream of a reason they'd try.
Putin said, with a grin,
he preferred that I win,
undermining my weak alibi.

Co-conspirator or useful dupe?
Either way, I'm in pretty thick soup.
How can I be acquitted?
My defense: I'm dim-witted!
Education makes my eyelids droop.

Comrade Putin I'll never betray.
I won't let the facts get in the way.
He has big dirt on me.
More than prostitute pee.
Laundered money will spell my doomsday.

WORDSMITH[92]
JULY 18, 2018

I mean wouldn't when stating it would,
And say bad when I'm thinking it's good.
When I get into trouble,
then my negatives double.
This is why I'm so misunderstood.

When attempting to walk my words back,
I resume my original tack.
People are taking bets
it's a form of Tourettes.
There's an impulse control that I lack.

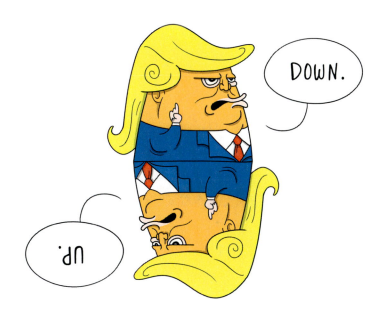

RECRUITIN' FOR PUTIN[93]
JULY 19, 2018

Putin hoped I'd exhibit the gall
to deliver him Michael McFaul.
He'd have been even prouder
if I sent him Bill Browder,
but the Senate caused this scheme to stall.

I so wanted to be Putin's hero,
but they shut me down 98-zero
I'll submit a new plan –
maybe send a new man.
How about if it's Robert DeNiro?[94]

Vlad would like me to deep-six Magnitsky,
to facilitate getting more rich-sky.
But to carry that out,
I'd need so much more clout
or a bunch of political hits-sky.

CAPITAL IDEA
JULY 22, 2018

Bolton said that to safeguard our nation,
I must seek Iran's capitulation.
But somehow I misheard,
and I thought the big word
that he used was "CAPITALIZATION."

Every once in awhile my brain snaps.
There are misfires across each synapse.
I'll be tweeting away,
sharing thoughts for the day
AND I'M SUDDENLY USING ALL CAPS!

Donald J. Trump
@realDonaldTrump

To Iranian President Rouhani: NEVER, EVER THREATEN THE UNITED STATES AGAIN OR YOU WILL SUFFER CONSEQUENCES THE LIKES OF WHICH FEW THROUGHOUT HISTORY HAVE EVER SUFFERED BEFORE. WE ARE NO LONGER A COUNTRY THAT WILL STAND FOR YOUR DEMENTED WORDS OF VIOLENCE & DEATH. BE CAUTIOUS!

8:24 PM · Jul 22, 2018

SUMMER CLEARANCE[96]
JULY 24, 2018

First Amendment expression is fine,
just so long as you toe the Trump line.
If you say that I'm wrong,
your tenure won't last long
and I'll make sure you're labeled as swine.

Criticism equals interference.
So use care in your TV appearance.
Brenner, Hayden and Clapper
are consigned to the crapper.
Denounce me and you'll forfeit your clearance.

DESTROYER LAWYER[97]
JULY 25, 2018

How could Cohen have deigned to record me?
He was loyal. Of that, he assured me!
We were birds of a feather,
being hoodlums together.
It's his criminal mind that allured me.

When you act like a mafia boss,
there are lines that your soldiers don't cross.
Cohen was a made man
in my Trump Nostra clan.
Now his carcass should fertilize moss.

HISTORIC DISTORTIONS[98]
JULY 27, 2018

It's a boom "of historic proportions."
This phrase better describes my distortions.
Since I'm not under oath,
I'll tout GDP growth
using false claims and mental contortions.

4.1 for one quarter's fantastic!
My connection to truth is elastic.
Not much chance we'll repeat it.
(And Obama did beat it.)
That won't stop me from being bombastic.

"ENEMY OF THE PEOPLE"[99]
AUGUST 3, 2018

A free press is our national foe.
I don't want information to flow.
It's a serious threat
to this marionette
in the Kremlin-controlled puppet show.

LEBRON[100]
AUGUST 4, 2018

I tweet racist taunts at snide LeBron
and that CNN anchor named Don.
Wouldn't toss them a crumb.
If they're black, then they're "dumb."
Not like geniuses at Q-Anon.

Unlike my bogus non-profit ploys,
LeBron actually helps girls and boys.
While I perpetrate fraud,
his work people applaud.
He's all action and I'm mostly noise.

CALIFORNIA WILDFIRES[101]
AUGUST 7, 2018

I don't need any facts to opine.
With my base that's entirely fine.
About fires I know zero.
I'll just fiddle like Nero,
while environment burns on the vine.

These huge wildfires could be averted
if they'd stop having rivers diverted
from the source to the sea.
This makes great sense to me!
Is my grasp of these concepts perverted?

I'm unable to fathom the notion
that the rivers flow into the ocean.
Start or end in the basin?
Depends which way you're facin'.
I don't get why this stirs such emotion.

Experts say that I have it ass backwards,
sort of like the pie inside the blackbirds,
or the hat in the cat,
the mouse chasing the rat,
or the lion pursued by the yak herds.

We can minimize burn devastation
with a good dose of deforestation.
I would solve it with ease:
just cut down all the trees.
Without fuel there is no conflagration.

Though my knowledge of science is fleeting,
I'll go on with nonsensical tweeting.
With no case to present,
my own truth I'll invent.
It's my personal form of excreting.

California wildfires are being magnified & made so much worse by the bad environmental laws which aren't allowing massive amounts of readily available water to be properly utilized. It is being diverted into the Pacific Ocean. Must also tree clear to stop fire from spreading!

2:53 PM - Aug 6, 2018

SPACE FARCE[102]
AUGUST 9, 2018

Why a super expensive "Space Force"?
To defend against Martians, of course!
And if stars can align
with Uranus (and mine),
we'll establish a great new gas source.

We'll commission the "Trump Battlestar,"
guarding galaxies both near and far.
We can capture Neptune,
put a base on the moon,
and make Mercury more than a car.

I'm excited about this endeavor.
And I think that this branding's real clever.
I'll build "Hotel Trump Venus"
in the shape of a penis,
and be known in the heavens forever.

 **Donald J. Trump** @realDonaldTrump

Space Force all the way!

9:03 AM - Aug 9, 2018

OMAROSA[103]
August 14, 2018

Omarosa is causing me strife.
Her disclosures cut through like a knife.
She was just one more cog
in my dank White House bog.
A reality TV "lowlife."

She lacked competence. That's why I fired her.
Had those same qualities when I hired her.
I bring only the best
and she passed that strict test
because fans of Apprentice admired her.

Pulled down one hundred eighty a year,
mostly sowing resentment and fear.
Rude behavior and lateness,
but she said I was GREATNESS,
so I told Kelly, "Please keep her here."

Placed my trust in that "dog" Manigault.
Now, as Jared might say, "Oy Gevalt!"
Conduct no one condones
from my ethics-starved clones.
But these screw-ups are never my fault.

Wacky Omarosa, who got fired 3 times on the Apprentice, now got fired for the last time. She never made it, never will. She begged me for a job, tears in her eyes, I said Ok. People in the White House hated her. She was vicious, but not smart. I would rarely see her but heard....

6:27 AM - Aug 13, 2018

...really bad things. Nasty to people & would constantly miss meetings & work. When Gen. Kelly came on board he told me she was a loser & nothing but problems. I told him to try working it out, if possible, because she only said GREAT things about me - until she got fired!

6:50 AM - Aug 13, 2018

Donald J. Trump @realDonaldTrump

When you give a crazed, crying lowlife a break, and give her a job at the White House, I guess it just didn't work out. Good work by General Kelly for quickly firing that dog!

4:31 AM - Aug 14, 2018

GIULIANI'S THEORY OF TRUTH RELATIVITY AND CONWAY'S COROLLARY[104]
AUGUST 19, 2018

Rudy teaches us truth isn't truth,
Sherlock Holmes wasn't much of a sleuth,
there's no blue in the sky,
a bluebird doesn't fly,
and a bicuspid isn't a tooth.

And what could one say to the contrary,
when presented Conway's corollary?
When you want to distract,
cite "alternative fact."
Of reality, always be wary.

MUELLER AND MCCARTHY[105]
AUGUST 19, 2018

There's so much that's the same about them!
After all, their names both start with M.
And McCarthy and Mueller
seem about the same color.
These twin villains I strongly condemn!

Donald J. Trump
@realDonaldTrump

Study the late Joseph McCarthy, because we are now in period with Mueller and his gang that make Joseph McCarthy look like a baby! Rigged Witch Hunt!

5:24 AM - Aug 19, 2018

BAD DAY AT BLACK ROCK[106]
(MEN OF CONVICTION)
AUGUST 21, 2018

I called Bob Mueller's team a "disgrace,"
and commented on Manafort's case.
I kept venting my fury.
Tried to influence the jury.
To me, that is a president's place.

But they found Paul was guilty on eight
and Mike's plea served my head on a plate.
Paul is such a "good man."
Hides his funds where he can.
Till he squealed on me, Mike was first rate.

I directed payoffs to some wench.
Now my "fixer" has thrown in a wrench.
Guilty verdicts and pleas.
I attract lice and fleas,
and my swamp spews a terrible stench.

The "witch hunt' keeps on locating witches.
I'm afraid they'll all turn into snitches.
I've consorted with crooks.
Will they open their books
and reveal the foul source of my riches?

FLIPPERS[107]
AUGUST 23, 2018

We should make it illegal to flip.
Something incriminating might slip.
If you rat on your boss,
you must suffer a loss.
Call it white collar crime censorship.
(How else can a kingpin hold his grip?)

PECKER[108]
AUGUST 24, 2018

Now it looks as though Pecker's been squeezed,
and the Trump haters all must be pleased.
What's our seminal plan
for this genital man?
Can I make sure his pressure is eased?

In the Trump team he's been a long member.
Now he's shrinking our chance in November.
Our deflation is rapid.
The campaign becomes flaccid.
The Trump fire is reduced to an ember.

It was such a strong bond that we forged,
but I've heard that his vault is engorged.
Can we try and make peace –
find another release,
before bountiful content's disgorged?

WEISSELBERG[109]
AUGUST 24, 2018

A subpoena to Al must be quashed.
He knows where all the money was washed,
where the bodies are buried,
where the chickens is curried,
every morsel I ever have noshed!

DISDAIN FOR MCCAIN[110]
AUGUST 28, 2018

My tribute to McCain was half-assed.
Wouldn't lower the flag to half-mast.
I am never enraptured
with a soldier who's captured
or whose legacy has me outclassed.

Since he left me frustrated and riled,
I'll behave like a petulant child.
He got into my head,
so I'm glad that he's dead
and I'll make sure his name is defiled.

I don't know why they thought I was rude,
but my tantrum got massively booed.
Though it caused me to gag,
I re-lowered the flag.
Now I'm nursing a miserable mood.

Will I lose my world leader credential
if I keep acting unpresidential?
Well, my base doesn't care.
They consider it flare.
Decent conduct is so non-essential.

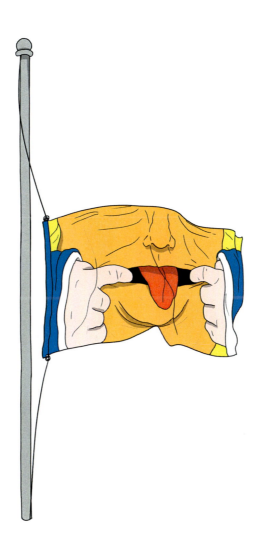

FUDGE![111]
AUGUST 30, 2018

From obstruction claims I need escape,
So I'll say Lester Holt fudged my tape.
Don't believe your own eyes.
It's just more "fake news" lies.
There's no truth that I cannot reshape.

Donald J. Trump
@realDonaldTrump

What's going on at @CNN is happening, to different degrees, at other networks - with @NBCNews being the worst. The good news is that Andy Lack(y) is about to be fired(?) for incompetence, and much worse. When Lester Holt got caught fudging my tape on Russia, they were hurt badly!

4:02 AM - Aug 30, 2018

IN THE ROUGH[112]
SEPTEMBER 1, 2018

After John McCain's stinging rebuff,
I'm alone hitting shots from the rough.
I'll just play golf and tweet
While the real leaders meet.
Of my rubbish they've all had enough.

FREE PASS FOR GOP CANDIDATES[113]
SEPTEMBER 3, 2018

People shouldn't be going to jail
if it means, in elections, I fail.
Don't care how they offended.
Justice must be suspended.
Run the law out of town on a rail!

If they're thugs and crooks, we must protect 'em.
Disregard their misdeeds and elect 'em.
Crime should carry no weight
(unless you immigrate).
That's the clear-sighted view from my rectum.

As foes circle my team like piranhas,
Trump Republic will grow more bananas.
I'll attack bedrock norms
till dictatorship forms.
And my quislings will shout their hosannas.

 Donald J. Trump
@realDonaldTrump

Two long running, Obama era, investigations of two very popular Republican Congressmen were brought to a well publicized charge, just ahead of the Mid-Terms, by the Jeff Sessions Justice Department. Two easy wins now in doubt because there is not enough time. Good job Jeff......

11:25 AM - Sep 3, 2018

INSIDER SHADING[114]
SEPTEMBER 5, 2018

They attack me in op-eds and books.
I'm not liking the way that it looks.
No one I know endorses
these anonymous sources
that keep springing from crannies and nooks.

Now they claim that a Trump appointee
wants to rescue the nation from me.
They can't pull such a scam.
Don't they know who I am?
Putting country first? That's treachery!

My insiders concede I'm unfit,
and I'll prove it by having a snit.
There's no one I can trust.
I'm about to combust.
They are writing my White House obit!

Rand Paul says everyone on my staff
should be hooked up to a polygraph.
It's a tactic worth trying.
Let's expose White House lying!
(Except all those told on my behalf.)

HOW TO EXPLAIN A HURRICANE[115]
SEPTEMBER 19, 2018

"It's real wet from the standpoint of water."
Slept through English at my alma mater.
Every time that I use it,
I assault and abuse it:
Massacre from the standpoint of slaughter.

Some have said I'm aspiring to be
a true master of tautology.
That's a word I'd resent
if I knew what it meant.
Language is such a mystery to me.

A SEX PREDATOR'S UNINFORMED ADVICE TO WOMEN[116]
SEPTEMBER 21, 2018

All true victims report the attack,
because people like me have their back.
If you quickly disclose
so that everyone knows,
you won't have to endure any flak.

If you're brutalized don't feel constraint.
Call the precinct and file your complaint.
You have only to gain.
There's no burden or pain.
You'll be hailed as a hero and saint.

Each attempted rape must be reported.
As a woman, you're always supported!
There is never a risk.
Vindication is brisk
and oppression is bound to be thwarted.

You should proceed without hesitation.
Who cares that they'll want corroboration,
and they'll smear your good name
and harass and defame
and subject you to humiliation.

I can offer these tips with great ease.
On this subject I have expertise.
Had these methods been used
by the ones I abused,
I'd be housed with Shawshank detainees.

 Donald J. Trump
@realDonaldTrump

I have no doubt that, if the attack on Dr. Ford was as bad as she says, charges would have been immediately filed with local Law Enforcement Authorities by either her or her loving parents. I ask that she bring those filings forward so that we can learn date, time, and place!

6:14 AM - Sep 21, 2018

TRUMPERY RHYMES

Vaguely Familiar Songs from the Nursery

LITTLE MISS DANIELS

Little Miss Daniels.
causing such scandals,
tormenting me each day.
Along comes Mike Cohen
to ask what we're owin'
and bargain Miss Daniels away.

THE FARMERS GO TO HELL

The farmers go to hell.
The farmers go to hell.
Tax China.
Ditch NAFTA.
And farmers go to hell.

BAA, BAA SESSIONS

Baa, baa Sessions.
Have you any soul?
No sir.
No sir.
Not my role!

TAX CUT BILL

Tax cut bill
went to the Hill,
fiscally under water.
Don't bat a lash.
We'll find the cash –
Send safety nets to slaughter.

HUMPTY TRUMPTY

Humpty Trumpty wants a big wall.
Humpty Trumpty's in for a fall.
All Mueller's horses
and all Mueller's men
will ensure Trumpty inhabits the pen.

I'M A BRITTLE DESPOT

I'm a brittle despot,
tall and stout.
Caught up in scandal,
wielding my clout.
Some say I'm a hustler
and a lout.
Criticize me and watch me pout.

DOWN BY THE LAPTOP

Down by the laptop
early in the morning.
See the little Twitter birdies
all in a row.
See the Twitter master
flying off the handle.
Tweet tweet, lie lie.
Off we go!

HERE'S HOW WE POUND OBAMA AND BUSH

Here's how we pound Obama and Bush.
Obama and Bush.
Obama and Bush.
Here's how we pound Obama and Bush,
so early in the morning.

This is the way we trash the press…

WITCHERY DITCHERY DOCK

Witchery ditchery dock.
Watch Mueller clean my clock.
The clock strikes one
and Flynn is done.
Witchery ditchery dock.

… The clock strikes two.
Gates gives in too.

… The clock strikes three.
Mike fingers me.

… The clock strikes four.
Paul gives them more …

SO PLAIN AND SO BORING

So plain and so boring.
Mike Pence leaves us snoring.
I went to bed,
a sick thought in my head:
He could be the new pres in the morning!

LOYAL MIKE FLYNN

Loyal Mike Flynn –
don't blow your horn.
I'll issue a pardon;
you'll be reborn.
Where's the smoking gun
I had you keep?
Under your back yard,
Buried deep.

FREAKY, SNEAKY PRUITT

The freaky, sneaky Pruitt
befouled the water spout,
brought acid rain
and dried the rivers out,
let sewage run,
then booked a first class plane,
and the freaky sneaky Pruitt
was never seen again.

CAN'T FIX IT. CAN'T MASK IT.

Can't fix it. Can't mask it.
I'm gonna blow a gasket.
Mike Cohen's gone and flipped on me
and now I've really lost it.

I've lost it. I've lost it.
Oh boy, I've really lost it.
I drew a red line in the sand
but Cohen went and crossed it.

MANAFORT IS IN A JAM

Manafort is in jam.
Legal jam.
Great big jam.
Why should he be in a jam?
He wasn't dealing snow!

OLD THE DONALD

Old The Donald has a swamp.
E-I-E-I-O.
Loves parades and lots of pomp,
though he's no G.I. Joe.
With a scandal here,
an indictment there.
Here a lie, there a lie,
everywhere a lie lie.
Old The Donald tends his swamp,
oozing from below

ENDNOTES

[1] On November 13, 2017, reports surface that during the course of his father's presidential campaign, Donald Trump Jr. was exchanging private messages with WikiLeaks, an organization long suspected of working closely with Russian intelligence services. WikiLeaks was publishing hacked emails of Democratic Party officials, including Hillary Clinton campaign chairman John Podesta. Within 15 minutes after Trump Jr. received one such message urging that he promote the hacked emails and attaching a link, his father tweets: "Very little pick-up by the dishonest media of incredible info provided by WikiLeaks. So dishonest! Rigged system!"

[2] In November 2017, nine women accuse Roy Moore (a former Chief Justice of the Alabama Supreme Court and now a Republican candidate for the U.S. Senate seat vacated by Jeff Sessions) of sexual misconduct. Three of the women allege that he sexually assaulted them when they were 16 years of age or younger. At the time of these alleged assaults, Moore was in his early thirties and serving as an assistant district attorney. A former manager of a mall in Gadsden, Alabama recalls that, due to complaints about Moore's sexual misconduct, he ordered Moore banned from the shopping center. The allegations surface after it is too late to remove Moore's name from the ballot. Moore, who professes to be deeply religious, denies the allegations. A number of prominent Republicans call for Moore to drop out of the race and still others withdraw their endorsement of his candidacy. Trump, who has numerous sexual misconduct accusers of his own, accepts Moore's denials and endorses him for the senate seat. (Moore also is famous for having twice defied federal law while serving as Chief Justice in Alabama. He was expelled from the Chief Justice position in November 2003 for refusing a federal court order to remove a marble monument of the Ten Commandments that he had placed in the court building. He again was elected Chief Justice in 2013, but was suspended three years later for defying a U.S. Supreme Court decision overturning a ban on same-sex marriage. In other words, Moore is Trump's kind of guy.) Ultimately, in a huge upset, Moore is defeated in the senate race by his Democratic opponent, Doug Jones.

[3] Demonstrating his usual sensitivity, at an event on November 27, 2017 honoring Navajo Code Talkers who served during World War II, Trump jokes, "You were here long before any of us were here. Although we have a representative in Congress who they say was here a long time ago. They call her Pocahontas." His reference is to Massachusetts Senator Elizabeth Warren, upon whom he derisively bestowed that nickname because of her claim to some Native American ancestry. Trump previously had been condemned by the National Congress of American Indians, the largest and oldest organization representing Native Americans, for referring to Senator Warren in that manner. In addition, this White House ceremony for the Code Talkers is held directly in front of a portrait of Andrew Jackson, who had signed the Indian Removal Act of 1830. That law resulted in the forced relocation of roughly 17,000 Cherokees from Georgia to present-day Oklahoma, in what has come to be known as the "Trail of Tears." Thousands died of cold, starvation and disease during that dangerous trek.

[4] On November 28, 2017, with a potential government shutdown looming due to failed budget talks, Senate Minority Leader Chuck Schumer and House Minority Leader Nancy Pelosi react to a Trump tweet by issuing a joint statement that they will not attend a scheduled bipartisan meeting that afternoon with the president. Trump's early morning tweet states, "Meeting with 'Chuck and Nancy' today about keeping government open and working. Problem is they want illegal immigrants flooding into our Country unchecked, are weak on Crime and want to substantially RAISE Taxes. I don't see a deal." The Schumer/Pelosi statement in response reads, "Given that the president doesn't see a deal between Democrats and the White House, we believe that the best path forward is to continue negotiating with our Republican counterparts in Congress instead."

[5] On November 29, 2017, in an early morning tweet which mentions the recent firing of Matt Lauer by NBC over allegations of sexual harassment, Trump takes a shot at Joe Scarborough, host of MSNBC's *Morning Joe*. His tweet says, "And will they terminate low ratings Joe Scarborough based on the 'unsolved mystery' that took place in Florida years ago? Investigate!" When Scarborough was a Republican congressman from Florida, his intern, Lori Klausutis, was found dead in his Florida district office. There is no proof that Scarborough had anything to do with her death. An autopsy report concluded that she had been feeling ill and that heart problems caused her to fall and hit her head. The Medical Examiner found no evidence of foul play.

[6] Also on the morning of November 29, 2017, Trump retweets three inflammatory anti-Muslim videos from a British far-right ultra-nationalist Twitter account. The videos depict purported Muslims assaulting people and, in one segment, smashing a statue of the Virgin Mary. Trump's retweets draw immediate and sharp condemnation from several British news websites and government officials. On the other hand, former Ku Klux Klan Grand Wizard David Duke heartily approves of Trump's actions, tweeting, "Thank God for Trump! That's why we love him!"

[7] On December 8, 2017, the Trump White House issues a proclamation declaring December 10, 2017 as Human Rights Day, in remembrance of those suffering under the "yolk" of authoritarianism and extremism. As a result of this announcement, many traumatized English teachers require emergency hospitalization. Twitter boils over in response: "This is what happens when you don't have enough eggheads on staff." "They're gonna have to scramble to fix it." "In another administration, someone would fry for this." "They're really dealing with a shell of a communications staff, not all of whom are eggcellent spellers." "I'll go over easy and give them the benedict of the doubt..."

[8] After having received approximately 20,000 fewer votes than his opponent in the special election for U.S. senator, Roy Moore refuses to concede, claiming "numerous reported cases of voter fraud." On December 28, 2017, Alabama's State Canvassing Board certifies the results, making Jones the first Democratic senator from that state in 25 years

[9] On December 12, 2017, New York Senator Kirsten Gillibrand, in a televised interview, says that in view of the numerous "credible allegations" against Trump of sexual assault, "he should be fully investigated and he should resign." Gillibrand also had called for the resignation of Democratic Senator Al Franken of Minnesota and opined that, in retrospect, former President Bill Clinton should have done the same. The next morning, Trump tweets, "Lightweight Senator Kirsten Gillibrand, a total flunky for Chuck Schumer and someone who would come to my office 'begging' for campaign contributions not so long ago (and would do anything for them), is now in the ring fighting against Trump. Very disloyal to Bill and Crooked – USED!" Gillibrand and various commentators regard Trump's remarks as sexist and as implying that Gillibrand would prostitute herself for campaign contributions. White House press secretary Sarah Huckabee Sanders states that Trump's comments are "in no way sexist" and would be considered so "only if your mind is in the gutter."

[10] More than a dozen women have accused Trump of groping and kissing them against their will, and he has denied each such allegation. In the infamous *Access Hollywood* tape, Trump boasts about his proclivity for such conduct and the fact that he can get away with it because of his celebrity. Trump's position concerning others facing such allegations appears to depend on their political affiliation and whether they support him. After news of allegations against Democratic Senator Al Franken, including a photograph of the senator pretending to fondle a woman while she is asleep, Trump mocks him in a tweet: "The Al Frankenstien (sic) picture is really bad, speaks a thousand words. Where do his hands go in pictures 2, 3, 4, 5 & 6 while she sleeps?" Upon learning of sexual harassment and assault allegations against movie mogul Harvey Weinstein, a Democrat, Trump states that he is "not surprised." Regarding the firing of NBC morning news host Matt Lauer for sexual harassment, Trump's reaction is to chide NBC for not also firing company executives for dispensing "fake news." In the past, Trump has been quick to support the credibility

of Bill Clinton's accusers, but has taken the position that the sexual harassment allegations against his own friend and cheerleader Bill O'Reilly are fabricated.

[11] By a strict party-line vote, Congress passes the Republican-sponsored tax overhaul plan, touted by Trump as an "early Christmas present." The sweeping plan substantially reduces the corporate tax rate and taxes for wealthy individuals, while providing moderate relief for middle income individuals. Despite reducing the top individual tax rate from 35 percent to 21 percent, Trump (who steadfastly has refused to disclose his own tax returns) claims this plan will not benefit him. The legislation also appears to retaliate against the population in states that voted for Hillary Clinton in the 2016 presidential election by capping what previously had been an unlimited deduction for state and local taxes at $10,000. The states that impose significant income and other taxes generally fall into the "blue" category. Some analysts conclude that the tax overhaul will increase the budget deficit by at least $2 trillion, but the administration argues that it will stimulate economic growth, thus ultimately offsetting the cost. It is clear, however, that the Republican-dominated Congress intends to find offsets by reducing spending on so-called "entitlement" programs that primarily benefit the poor.

[12] At a meeting with senior agency officials who oversee the budget, Centers for Disease Control and Prevention (CDC) policy analysts are advised of a list of forbidden terms. Those terms are "vulnerable," "entitlement," "diversity," "transgender," "fetus," "evidence-based," and "science-based." The ban applies to budget and supporting documents that are to be given to CDC's partners and to Congress. The analysts are not given any reason for the word ban.

[13] See note 11. With great fanfare, Trump signs the "tax reform" legislation on December 22, 2017.

[14] Apparently in response to Trump's taunting tweets, North Korea fires more test missiles in the ensuing days.

[15] During a press conference on January 6, 2018, when asked about a *New York Times* story which reported that he had ordered White House counsel Don McGahn to pressure Attorney General Jeff Sessions not to recuse himself from the Russia investigation, Trump states, "Everything that I've done was 100 percent proper. That's what I do is I do things proper." Trump calls the *Times* story "way off, or at least off." He also continues to insist that there was no collusion between his campaign and Russia.

[16] In early January 2018, author Michael Wolff publishes his book entitled *Fire and Fury: Inside the Trump White House*, which details the early days in the Trump administration and paints an extremely unflattering portrait of the president and his staff. The book, which purports to be based on numerous interviews with staff and Wolff's unfettered access to daily White House activities over several months, portrays the administration as dysfunctional and paralyzed by infighting. Lawyers for Trump unsuccessfully try to block the book's publication, arguing that it would violate a confidentiality agreement. Spokesperson Sarah Sanders characterizes the book as "trashy tabloid fiction." The book immediately sails to number one on the best seller list.

[17] In a meeting in the Oval Office on January 11, 2018, a group of lawmakers discuss with Trump a possible budget resolution that addresses immigration issues, including protection of immigrants from Haiti, El Salvador and African countries. According to sources present at the meeting, Trump responds by asking, "Why are we having people from shithole countries come here?" Trump then suggests that the United States should instead accept more people from countries such as Norway, whose prime minister visited the day before. Trump also singles out Haiti, stating, "Why do we need more Haitians? Take them out." In November, the Trump administration had rescinded deportation protection granted to almost 60,000 Haitian refugees following the 2010 earthquake and ordered that they return home by July 2019.

[18] The *Wall Street Journal* triggers a new scandal for Trump when it reports that his lawyer, Michael Cohen, paid porn star Stormy Daniels $130,000 to remain quiet about a sexual relationship they had in 2006. The

hush payment was made shortly before the 2016 presidential election. *Mother Jones* reports that, according to emails between political operatives who were advising Daniels in 2009, the porn actress had described some of Trump's unusual behavior during their fling, including making her spank him with a copy of *Forbes* magazine featuring Trump on the cover. The alleged affair with Daniels occurred while Melania Trump was pregnant. This is not the only time hush money had been paid to suppress stories of Trump's extramarital trysts. In November 2016 the *Wall Street Journal* reported that the *National Enquirer*, owned by Trump's friend David Pecker, had paid *Playboy* magazine centerfold Karen McDougal $150,000 for the rights to her account of a 10-month affair with Trump, then buried the story by failing to publish it.

[19] As the deadline to avoid a government shutdown looms, Trump continues to demand an agreement to fund his border wall ($18 billion to fund only half of it, according to the *Wall Street Journal*) and the Democrats continue to demand restoration of the DACA program for young immigrants brought to the United States as children (also known as "Dreamers"). After the meeting earlier in January in which Trump undercut efforts at compromise on immigration with his reference to "shithole countries" (see note 17), Republican congressional leaders, including Senator Lindsey Graham of South Carolina and Senate Majority Leader Mitch McConnell, bemoan Trump's lack of clarity on what kind of deal he will approve. Reports surface that White House aide Stephen Miller, with his strong anti-immigration stance, keeps throwing a wrench in the works regarding that issue. On Friday, January 19, 2018, in a last ditch effort to avert a shutdown, Trump asks Senate Minority Leader Chuck Schumer to attend a private lunch meeting at the White House. During their discussion, Schumer "reluctantly" agrees to some funding toward construction of the border wall and Trump agrees, in exchange, to support legal protection for Dreamers. Schumer leaves the meeting also believing that Trump will support a three to four day extension to finalize an agreement, but subsequent phone calls from Trump and his chief of staff John Kelly demonstrate White House retrenchment on both the short-term extension and the immigration issue. Just before the midnight deadline, Trump tweets, "Dems want a Shutdown in order to diminish the great success of the Tax Cuts, and what they are doing for our booming economy." Schumer, on the Senate floor, blames Trump for abandoning a deal that was within reach. Trump leaves for a weekend of golf and fundraising in Mar-a-Lago.

[20] In February 2018 the *Washington Post* breaks a story that last April, Trump told White House counsel Don McGahn to call the Justice Department and ask a senior official to convince then-FBI director James Comey to publicly exonerate him in the Russia probe. Trump also had personally appealed to Comey to clear his name. In response to Trump's request, McGahn did contact then-Deputy Acting Attorney General Dana Boente, who did not follow up. This revelation comes as Special Counsel Robert Mueller continues to investigate whether Trump attempted to obstruct justice in connection with Mueller's inquiry into Russian election interference. McGahn spent two days interviewing in Mueller's office in December. McGahn again was in the limelight in January, when the *New York Times* reported that, according to White House officials, he had threatened to resign when Trump asked him to fire Robert Mueller last June. Meanwhile, Mueller's office has been negotiating with Trump's attorneys about interviewing the president. While Trump tells reporters he would welcome such an interview, his lawyers push to avoid that scenario, likely out of concern that the president, who has a penchant for embellishment, exaggeration and outright lying, could be charged with perjury.

[21] On February 2, 2018, the Republican-controlled House Intelligence Committee releases to the public, over the objections of its Democrat members, a four-page memo authored by its chairman, Devin Nunes, a staunch Trump ally. The memo asserts that a group of politically motivated FBI agents abused the Foreign Intelligence Surveillance Act (FISA) warrant process for the purpose of undermining the Trump presidency, including excessive and improper dependence on the Trump-Russia dossier, an unverified report prepared by private investigator Christopher Steele. That dossier was funded, in part, by the Hillary Clinton campaign and the Democratic National Committee. Trump and his political allies argue that the memo discredits the Mueller investigation into Russian interference with the 2016 election. Trump approves release of the memo over strong objections from the FBI (including Christopher Wray, Trump's appointee to replace James

Comey as its director) and the intelligence community. The FBI issues a statement expressing "grave concerns" about factual omissions and inaccuracies in the Nunes memo, as well as potential exposure and resulting compromise of intelligence sources and methods. Democrats prepare a 10-page rebuttal to the Nunes memo. Publication of that rebuttal initially is blocked by Trump pending redaction of any classified and sensitive material. A redacted version of the rebuttal finally is released on February 24. The rebuttal points out, among other things, that the dossier was only one of several evidentiary pieces submitted with the warrant applications and that those applications did disclose the partisan funding of the dossier. Additionally, each of the FISA judges approving these warrants was a Republican appointee.

[22] In a tweet containing characteristic spelling errors, Trump falsely claims that the Nunes memo vindicates him in the Russia probe. He also, without basis, states that the probe has failed to uncover collusion or obstruction of justice.

[23] In a speech in Cincinnati on February 5, 2018, Trump expresses his displeasure at the fact that Democrats failed to stand and applaud at his State of the Union address the previous week. Specifically, he is referring to the unenthusiastic response of the Congressional Black Caucus to his highly questionable claim of credit for a low unemployment rate among African Americans. Trump declares: "They were like death and un-American. Un-American. Somebody said, 'treasonous.' I mean, yeah, I guess why not? Can we call that treason? Why not? I mean they certainly didn't seem to love our country that much."

[24] Trump tells the Pentagon he wants a military parade "like the one in France." Trump had expressed great admiration for the Bastille Day parade when he visited that country last year. His directive to the Pentagon comes days before the planned North Korean military parade scheduled for February 8, 2018, at which it is anticipated the country's new long-range ballistic missiles will be prominently displayed.

[25] On February 7, 2018, it is announced that top White House aide Rob Porter will resign after physical abuse allegations by his two ex-wives were made public, including, most notably, a photograph of one of them with a swollen and badly bruised eye. The White House was made aware of those allegations in November but failed to act on them. In fact, largely because of the abuse allegations, Porter had been unable to receive a full security clearance from the FBI. As Trump's staff secretary, Porter earns the highest salary level in the White House and has regular access to sensitive and classified information. Various government officials express concern and disbelief that Porter was permitted to remain in this job without security clearance. Porter also is dating White House communications director Hope Hicks. White House press secretary Sarah Sanders refuses to comment on Porter's security clearance status, says Porter is "someone of the highest integrity and exemplary character," and states that in order to ensure a smooth transition, he will not be leaving his post immediately. White House chief of staff John Kelly also praises Porter as "a man of integrity and honor."

[26] On February 9, 2018, at the winter Olympics opening ceremony, Vice President Pence stands for the American flag as it passes but chooses to sit for every other nation's flag. Last October, Pence attended, also at taxpayer expense, a football game between the Indianapolis Colts and San Francisco 49ers, with instructions from Trump to leave the game if any players kneeled during the national anthem. Predictably, that scenario played out and Pence abruptly left the game before it started. Pence also now claims, incredibly, that he "just learned" about the domestic abuse allegations against White House aide Rob Porter, even though the administration was notified of the matter last November. This is reminiscent of Pence's less than credible denial of knowledge regarding former national security advisor Michael Flynn's conversations with Russian operatives. As these verses are written in Trump's voice, one must suspend judgment as to whether he would know the word "obsequious."

[27] According to a report in the *Washington Post*, Trump has refrained from reading the President's Daily Brief during his first year in office, breaking with the practice of his last seven predecessors. This classified document describes the most pressing issues of the day, collected by intelligence officials around the world. An administration official states that reading is not Trump's preferred "style of learning" and that he instead

relies on oral briefings augmented with photos, videos and colorful graphics. Trump also has told reporters that he is too busy to read, but he is known to carve out what he calls "executive time" to watch cable television news, primarily the conservative Fox News Channel.

[28] On February 14, 2018 – Valentine's Day – a gunman enters Marjory Stoneman Douglas High School in Parkland, Florida, an affluent suburb approximately 30 miles northwest of Fort Lauderdale, and shoots 34 people, using an AR-15 style rifle and multiple ammunition magazines. Fourteen students and three staff members are killed. An armed school resource officer of the Broward County Sheriff's Office is on campus at the time but remains outside and does not confront the shooter. The suspect, 19-year old former student Nikolas Cruz, is apprehended shortly after escaping the scene. Cruz had been expelled from the school and was reported to have had psychiatric and anger management issues. Local law enforcement had received prior tips about his potential danger to the community. Republican politicians, many of whom have received large financial contributions from the National Rifle Association (NRA), react to the shooting in typical fashion, offering prayers and condolences, focusing on the role of mental health, and dodging discussion of gun control as either too political or "too soon." The NRA, as usual, doubles down, citing the Second Amendment and arguing that people and not guns are the problem.

[29] The day after the Parkland shooting, Trump speaks to the nation. Using a teleprompter and sticking to his prepared text, he mentions praying for and comforting the grieving and wounded. He talks about shock, pain, and searching for answers. He says, "I want to speak now directly to America's children, especially those who feel lost, alone, confused, or even scared: I want you to know that you are never alone and you never will be. You have people who care about you, who love you, and who will do anything at all to protect you. If you need help, turn to teachers, a family member, a local police officer, or a faith leader. Answer hate with love; answer cruelty with kindness. We must also work together to create a culture in our country that embraces the dignity of life, that creates deep and meaningful human connections and that turns classmates and colleagues into friends and neighbors." He says he is committed to "working with state and local leaders to help secure our schools, and tackle the difficult issue of mental health." He prays for "healing and peace." He makes no mention whatsoever of stricter gun control laws.

[30] On February 16, 2018, a federal indictment is issued against 13 Russian nationals in connection with Robert Mueller's probe into election interference. The indictment names, among others, a wealthy restauranteur linked to Russian President Vladimir Putin. The businessman allegedly paid for the operation that created fictitious media accounts and used them to spread messages hurtful to the Clinton campaign. This operation, also called a "troll farm" or "troll factory," was headquartered in St. Petersburg, Russia and aimed at either influencing voters or undermining their faith in the U.S. political system, according to the 37-page indictment. The indictment alleges that, along with producing social media posts supporting Trump's candidacy and disparaging Clinton's, the organization purchased online advertisements using identities stolen from Americans, staged political rallies while posing as American activists, and paid people to promote or ridicule the candidates. American participants in this particular scheme are described as probably "unwitting." This indictment does not address other allegations of Russian interference, such as the hacking of Clinton emails, nor does it address potential collusion by the Trump campaign.

[31] On February 22, 2018, a little over a week following the Parkland gun massacre, Trump tweets his unwavering support for and praise of the NRA, then proposes his solution to school safety: arming teachers. Trump tells state and local officials, who are gathered at the White House to discuss school safety, that teachers could carry concealed weapons and "nobody would know who they are." He also says that teachers would go through "rigorous training" and could get "a little bit of a bonus." In a later tweet, he touts arming teachers as a "GREAT DETERRENT!" Teacher organizations and many individual teachers immediately speak out in opposition to this proposal, noting that armed combat is not their job, that first responders could confuse a gun-toting teacher with the perpetrator, and that having a loaded gun in the classroom can have unintended lethal consequences. Meanwhile, as surviving Parkland students become visible and active in promoting gun control legislation, right-wing commentators and NRA supporters begin a

campaign to smear them. Conspiracy theorist Alex Jones proclaims that outspoken student David Hogg is a paid actor, and this false claim goes viral on the internet.

[32] At a meeting with the nation's governors on February 26, 2018, Trump claims that he would have rushed in to aid students and teachers during the deadly Parkland shooting: "You don't know until you're tested but I think, I really believe, I'd run in there even if I didn't have a weapon, and I would think most of the people in this room would have done that too." He contrasts his presumed bravery with the actions of officers who failed to stop the gunman, saying, "They really weren't exactly Medal of Honor winners." He fails to note that, having avoided military service entirely due to alleged bone spurs, he never became a Medal of Honor winner either.

[33] In a surprise announcement on February 28, 2018, White House communications director Hope Hicks says she will be leaving her post in the coming weeks. Hicks, a former model who joined Trump's presidential campaign without any political experience, became known as someone who had the president's ear and could challenge him to change his views. The announcement of her resignation comes one day after she testified for eight hours before the House Intelligence Committee in connection with its investigation into Russian interference with the election. Reportedly, she told the panel that in her job, she occasionally had been required to tell "white lies" but never had lied about anything related to the Russia probe. Hicks also is the latest girlfriend of Rob Porter, who recently resigned his White House position due to publicized allegations of spousal abuse. Trump issues a statement praising Hicks and saying he will miss her.

[34] In his continuing feud with Attorney General Jeff Sessions over what he believes was Sessions' unnecessary recusal from the Russia investigation, Trump tweets that his attorney general's conduct in the White House has been "disgraceful." Trump's latest criticism centers primarily on Sessions' decision to ask the FBI's Inspector General to investigate Republican allegations of FISA abuse in surveilling Trump associates as part of the Russia investigation. Trump suggests that instead he should have used Justice Department lawyers. When asked by reporters if he still has confidence in Sessions, Trump routinely has ducked the question. Responding to Trump's latest criticism, Sessions issues a statement in which he says, "As long as I am Attorney General, I will continue to discharge my duties with integrity and honor." *Newsweek* reports that Trump's private nickname for Sessions is "Mr. Magoo," after the vision-impaired cartoon character of the 1950s.

[35] On March 1, 2018, Trump announces his intention to impose a 25 percent tariff on steel and a 10 percent tariff on aluminum imports. In a tweet the next day, Trump states, "Trade wars are good, and easy to win." Trump's announcement comes against the advice of many economic experts and even some members of his own administration, including chief economic advisor Gary Cohn. Stock prices dive in reaction. A survey of leading economists reveals a consensus that imposing new tariffs on these products will not improve the welfare of Americans and, in fact, is likely to have the opposite effect. They will increase the cost of consumer goods. The tariff on steel will harm workers in American industries that use steel, who outnumber those working in steel-producing jobs by approximately 80 to 1. Although large American steel and aluminum producers might initially benefit, small and middle-sized ones who rely on foreign materials might struggle due to the tariffs. A study indicates that Trump's tariff proposal would lead to the loss of an estimated 146,000 jobs, with greater job losses if other countries retaliate by imposing tariffs on American products. Forty-five U.S. trade associations urge Trump not to impose these tariffs on China, warning that it would be particularly harmful to the American economy and consumers.

[36] Inspired by the constant barrage of lies in Trump's tweets, rallies and statements to the press, some bloggers and news organizations maintain a running tally. The falsity of many statements is easily provable. While the fact that he lies is beyond dispute, some commentators opine that since he frequently contradicts his own statements, he might not even realize he is lying and that while pathological, it might be unintentional.

[37] News outlets report that Housing and Urban Development (HUD) Secretary Ben Carson was found to have spent $31,000 in taxpayer money on a new dining table and chairs for his Washington, D.C. office, exceeding the $5000 federal limit on office décor. A former HUD official, Helen Foster, alleges that she was reassigned because she raised concerns about the purchase. In a statement, Carson says he initially was unaware of the purchase. A HUD spokesperson says that the agency will attempt to "rescind" the furniture order. Not only does the discovery of this purchase raise ethics concerns, it also causes controversy in light of the agency's proposed budget cuts, which are substantial and would negatively impact health and human services. Treasury Secretary Steve Mnuchin and Environmental Protection Agency director Scott Pruitt also have been embroiled in scandals over their extravagant expenditure of public funds for their own private benefit and comfort.

[38] Former Trump aide Sam Nunberg, who was hired, then departed, then was rehired only to be let go again, is subpoenaed by Robert Mueller's investigative team to testify before a grand jury and to provide reams of documents, including emails. He had been a key strategic architect early in the Trump campaign. On Monday, March 7, 2018, Nunberg spends virtually the entire day being interviewed by reporters from various news networks, appearing disheveled and manic. At one point he is asked by CNN's Erin Burnett whether he has been drunk during television appearances, which he vehemently denies. In these interviews Nunberg flatly insists that he will not comply with Mueller's subpoena. At the end of the day, however, after repeatedly having been reminded by reporters that such disobedience could result in jail time, he changes his mind. As in other instances where individuals associated with his campaign have been targeted by Mueller's investigation, Trump tries to distance himself from Nunberg, claiming he was a minor player.

[39] Mueller already has indicted former Trump chief of staff Michael Flynn and former campaign chairman Paul Manafort, and is reported to be investigating Trump ally Roger Stone's connections with Russian nationals and his communications with WikiLeaks founder Julian Assange.

[40] Reports reveal that Trump's son-in-law Jared Kushner unsuccessfully had sought a half billion dollar loan from a Qatar-based investor for the Kushner family real estate business, a negotiation that continued after Trump became president and Kushner assumed a high ranking role in the administration. The deal fell apart in April 2017. Just a few weeks later, several Persian Gulf nations, including Saudi Arabia, the United Arab Emirates and Egypt, announced a blockade against Qatar over the latter's alleged terrorism links. On Twitter, Trump claims credit for the blockade, citing his recent meetings in the Middle East with these nations.

[41] Turnover in the Trump administration is high. More than one in three top White House officials left by the end of Trump's first year in office and fewer than half of the 12 positions closest to the president are still occupied by those who were present at the beginning, according to a study by the Brookings Institution. Very recent departure announcements include Rob Porter and Hope Hicks, and more are rumored.

[42] On March 6, 2017, Trump's top economic advisor Gary Cohn announces that he will resign, becoming the latest in a series of high-profile departures. Cohn had advocated against Trump's decision to impose steel and aluminum tariffs and had warned that he might resign if Trump insisted on implementing them.

[43] See notes 41 and 42. Trump denies that there is any problem.

[44] On March 12, 2018, Trump abandons his promise to work for certain gun control measures opposed by the NRA. In February, after the Parkland school shooting, Trump had announced on live television that he would push to raise the age limit for purchasing rifles to age 21 and would support strengthening background checks. He later told lawmakers (including Pennsylvania Senator Pat Toomey) that while the NRA has "great power over you people, they have less power over me." Reversing his ground, Trump now says that these matters should be left to the states. He also releases a modest plan that is more consistent with that of the NRA and its executive vice president, Wayne LaPierre. This plan would provide weapons training for teachers and create a commission to study other responses to school shootings. Trump

previously has made fun of the notion of establishing commissions, declaring them a waste of time and resources.

[45] On March 13, 2018, Trump fires his secretary of state, Rex Tillerson, and announces that he will be replaced by CIA director Mike Pompeo, who formerly served as a Tea Party congressman. Tillerson learns of his firing when a top aide shows him a tweet from the president announcing the change. While Tillerson had clashed openly and repeatedly with Trump over his approach to foreign policy, Pompeo is perceived as more in sync with the president's nationalist agenda. Tillerson's position at the White House appeared tenuous as of last October, when news reports surfaced that he had referred to Trump as a "fucking moron" during a Pentagon meeting. Tillerson never denied the "moron" comment. In his tweet concerning the departure, Trump thanks Tillerson for his service and also names Gina Haspel, a CIA operative, to replace Pompeo as the new CIA director.

[46] On March 15, 2018 (the Ides of March), the *Washington Post* reports that, according to numerous White House sources, Trump is dissatisfied with national security advisor H.R. McMaster and intends to fire him, but will defer such action "to ensure both that the three-star Army general is not humiliated and that there is a strong successor lined up." Apparently, Trump has told enough members of his administration about his plan to fire McMaster that they feel comfortable making this public disclosure. Of course, this leaves McMaster twisting in the wind and, most likely, humiliated. Just two days earlier Trump humiliated his secretary of state, firing him by tweet. (See note 45.) This revelation about McMaster, combined with the recent departure of several top administrators and rumors of more shakeups, has White House staff on edge. Trump reportedly has joked to those around him, "Who's next?"

[47] Robert Mueller's investigation continues unabated and without leaks. The only real disclosures about the progress of the probe are through public court filings, including indictments against top Trump campaign officials and Russian oligarchs. Trump continues to maintain that his campaign did not collude with Russia to tip the election in his favor and repeatedly asserts, without basis, that the Mueller team has confirmed his innocence. In the meantime it is known that Trump and his compatriots had close contacts with Russian oligarchs during the course of the election campaign, some of whom obtained and illegally distributed hacked emails belonging to the Democratic Party in an effort to help Trump win. It also is evident that Trump had strong financial ties to Russia, with his loans from oligarchs resulting in significant debt. Russia wanted sanctions lifted (a move advocated by Trump) and Trump presumably wanted both debt relief and help winning the election. In other words, it is not difficult to discern a collusive *quid pro quo*. From all indications, this is one thread of the Mueller investigation, which does not please the president.

[48] Trump's affair with porn star Stormy Daniels, and his attempts to silence her concerning it, dominates the news and keeps getting more bizarre. Daniels alleges that she and Trump had sexual relations beginning in 2006. Trump, through his lawyer/fixer Michael Cohen and his press secretary Sarah Sanders, denies it. Trump himself does not directly address the issue. Cohen does admit to having paid Daniels $130,000 to keep quiet but is cagey about whether Trump was aware of such payment or reimbursed him for it. To make the payment, Cohen set up a private Delaware company and used fictitious names for all involved. In exchange for the payment, Daniels signed a nondisclosure agreement (which never was signed by Trump, either under his real name or his *nom de guerre*). Daniels, however, is not remaining silent despite Cohen's threats to sue her for as much as $20 million for breaching an agreement his client never signed. She makes numerous public statements about the matter and is now scheduled to appear on *60 Minutes*. In terms of media savvy, Trump may have met his match.

[49] On March 18, 2018, Russian President Vladimir Putin wins re-election to a fourth six-year term amid widespread allegations of ballot box stuffing and forced voting. Despite admonishments from his national security advisors not to congratulate Putin, Trump does so anyway in a phone call two days after the election. Trump's gesture comes at a time when tensions are high between the Kremlin and the West due to a nerve gas attack on a former Russian double agent living in England and increasing evidence of

Russia's election meddling and infrastructure hacking. "An American president does not lead the Free World by congratulating dictators on winning sham elections," Senator John McCain of Arizona says in a statement. Critics continue to question Trump's motives for his constant flattering of Putin.

[50] On March 22, 2018, Trump carries out his threat to target China with trade sanctions, announcing approximately $50 billion in annual tariffs on a variety of Chinese goods. As expected, China responds that it will retaliate by implementing tariffs on U.S. agricultural products such as soybeans, which have a large market in China. The stock markets, which have been shaky since Trump's announcement of tariffs on steel and aluminum weeks earlier, now take a nose dive, with the Dow plunging 724 points in a single day.

[51] A day after presidential press secretary Sarah Sanders tells reporters she is unaware of any impending change regarding the national security advisor position, Trump names John R. Bolton to replace H.R. McMaster. Bolton is a hawkish former American ambassador to the United Nations who has called for military action against Iran and North Korea. It is reported that Bolton had been on the list of candidates for this post since the beginning of the administration, but that Trump hesitated, in part, because he disliked Bolton's walrus-like mustache. Instead of telling McMaster of his ouster face-to-face, Trump places an office-to-office phone call.

[52] Apparently in reaction to a segment on Fox News bearing the headline, "Caravan of Illegal Immigrants Headed to the U.S.," Trump follows up a "Happy Easter" tweet with a barrage decrying immigrant flow across the southern border, threatening to stop the North American Free Trade Agreement (NAFTA) and declaring that there will be no deal on the Deferred Action for Childhood Arrivals (DACA) program. The DACA program was begun during the Obama administration to provide temporary protection for so-called "Dreamers" who were brought here as children. Trump canceled the program in the fall but said he would be willing to reach a deal with Congress to reinstate those protections in exchange for funding to build his long-promised border wall (the one for which he had promised Mexico would pay). He went on, however, to reject related proposals from congressional Democrats (see note 19).

[53] Sinclair Broadcast Group, the largest owner of local television stations in the U.S., is politically conservative and pro-Trump in its news programming. During the 2016 presidential campaign, Sinclair stations gave a disproportionate amount of neutral and favorable coverage to Trump as compared with its coverage of Hillary Clinton. Also, according to *Politico*, Trump's son-in-law Jared Kushner disclosed to a group of business executives that their campaign had an agreement with Sinclair to give it access to Trump, provided that the interviews be broadcast without commentary. In March 2018, Sinclair news anchors nationwide read a one-minute long script that sounds much like Trump himself, attacking what it characterizes as "irresponsible, one-sided" and "fake" stories produced by other news outlets. When a media backlash ensues against this Sinclair-mandated spot, Trump defends the company, saying Sinclair is "far superior" to news outlets such as CNN and "fake NBC, which is a total joke." Meanwhile, Sinclair is attempting to expand its already dominant local market coverage by acquiring Tribune Media's 42 television stations, a move that would place it in 72 percent of the nation's households. Such media consolidations require approval by the Federal Communications Commission (FCC) which, under current Trump-friendly leadership, is easing rules that disfavor this type of merger. At the same time, Trump continues to loudly oppose a merger between Time Warner (the parent company of CNN, which Trump repeatedly maligns as "fake news") and AT&T.

[54] Trump continues his long-running and mostly one-sided feud with Jeff Bezos, who in October 2017 became the world's wealthiest man. Bezos is indirect owner of the *Washington Post*, a newspaper which has criticized Trump's words and actions. Bezos also is the founder of Amazon. In a series of tweets, Trump attacks Amazon, alleging that it pays "little or no" taxes to state and local government and is "putting many thousands of retailers out of business!" Trump also claims that Amazon is using the U.S. Postal Service "as their Delivery Boy," resulting in huge monetary losses to the country. As is often the case with

Trump's assertions, there is no evidence to support the statement that the Postal Service discount, given in exchange for the enormous amount of business Amazon provides, has caused a financial loss.

[55] On April 2, 2018, China retaliates against Trump's steel and aluminum tariffs by imposing tariffs of its own on imported U.S. products, including pork

[56] EPA administrator Scott Pruitt becomes the subject of numerous allegations of ethics violations and profligate spending of taxpayer dollars, including his frequent first class travel, his sweetheart deal to rent a condominium from the wife of an energy lobbyist, his millions of dollars in expenditures on a 20-member full-time security detail that is three times the size of his predecessor's part-time contingent, large pay raises reportedly given to his top aides without White House approval, and directing his personal driver to use a siren while traveling through traffic. Pruitt has been carrying out aggressively Trump's agenda of reducing environmental regulation and enforcement. In response to the growing uproar over Pruitt's spending and questionable ethics, press secretary Sanders tells reporters that the White House is "continuing to review any of the concerns that we have." Meanwhile, multiple administration officials tell news outlets that the president is considering replacing Attorney General Jeff Sessions with Pruitt. In response to this revelation, Trump tweets on April 6, 2018, "Do you believe that the Fake News Media is pushing hard on a story that I am going to replace A.G. Jeff Sessions with EPA Chief Scott Pruitt, who is doing a great job but is TOTALLY under siege?"

[57] On April 5, 2018, answering reporter questions on Air Force One, Trump says he did not know that his personal attorney Michael Cohen paid porn star Stormy Daniels $130,000 days before the election to prevent her from publicly accusing him of having an affair with her. Trump also denies knowing where Cohen got the money for the payment. He refuses to comment on whether he had set up a fund for Cohen to cover expenses like this. Later in the day, Daniels' attorney Michael Avenatti tweets, "The strength of our case [for invalidating the non-disclosure agreement] just went up exponentially. You can't have an agreement when one party claims to know nothing about it." Daniels already has spoken extensively about the matter anyway, including on a segment of *60 Minutes*.

[58] On April 7, 2018, a fire on the 50th floor of the New York City Trump Tower leaves a 67-year old resident dead and six firefighters injured. It is the second fire to occur in the building in 2018. The building, which was constructed in 1984, does not have sprinklers on its residential floors. A sprinkler requirement in new buildings did not take effect until 1999. Trump, then a private citizen, initially lobbied against the sprinkler mandate before it was adopted. He withdrew his opposition when it became clear that owners of existing buildings, such as his, only would be required to install a sprinkler system if they underwent gut renovations. At the time, he said that he understood sprinklers made residents "feel safer." After the fatal fire, Trump tweets glowingly about how well-constructed the building is. He makes no mention of the deceased resident.

[59] On April 9, 2018, federal investigators execute a "no knock" search warrant at attorney Michael Cohen's office and hotel room. Trump responds by calling it "an attack on our country," a characterization he studiously has avoided using for the Russian interference in the 2016 presidential election. The next morning, he tweets, "Attorney-client privilege is dead!" Then, a moment later, he tweets, "A TOTAL WITCH HUNT!!!" A no knock warrant authorizes entry without warning, including forced entry, to prevent destruction of evidence. Judges require an elevated showing of probable cause to authorize such warrants, including not only demonstration of the likelihood that evidence of a crime will be discovered, but also reason to suspect such evidence will be destroyed in the absence of surprise. Trump presumably is concerned that the records of his long-time attorney and fixer, including emails and possibly tapes, will incriminate Trump as to one aspect or another of the Mueller probe.

[60] On the eve of publication of former FBI director James Comey's book entitled *A Higher Loyalty*, in which the president is described as "untethered to the truth," Trump unleashes tweets attacking him. While slamming Comey for allegedly lying under oath and leaking classified information, Trump pardons Lewis

"Scooter" Libby, a former aide to President George W. Bush who, in 2007, was convicted of perjury and obstruction of justice in connection with the FBI's investigation to determine the source of a leak of classified information that resulted in compromising the identity of CIA officer Valerie Plame. It was Comey who, while serving as a top Justice Department official, appointed Libby's prosecutor. Libby long ago had completed serving his sentence. The pardon sends a clear message to former Trump campaign officials and members of the Trump administration who are currently embroiled in the Mueller investigation and indictments stemming from it. On the other hand, pardoning targets of the investigation will not protect Trump against documentary evidence such as that found in written records and audio recordings.

[61] On May 2, 2018, Rudolph W. Giuliani, former mayor of New York City who now serves as one of Trump's lawyers, says during an interview on Fox News that the president funneled the Stormy Daniels hush money reimbursement to Michael Cohen using a fund set up for these kinds of payments. "The president repaid it," Giuliani states. Rather than a one-time reimbursement of $130,000, Giuliani asserts, it was split into smaller retainer payments "with a little profit and a little margin for paying taxes." According to Giuliani, Trump "didn't know about the specifics of it … but he did know about the general arrangement – that Michael would take care of things like this, like I take care of things like this for my clients." Giuliani's version directly contradicts Trump's statement on Air Force One in early April that he did not know where Cohen got the money for the payment. On May 3, 2018, contrary to his own earlier denial that he knew about the hush money, Trump backs up Giuliani's statements in a series of tweets. The next day, Trump seems to backtrack, saying that "Giuliani is a great guy but he just started a day ago" and is "learning the subject matter" and "he'll get his facts straight." Trump dodges the question of when he learned that the Cohen "retainer" payments were used to pay off Daniels, saying, "You're going to find out, because we're going to give a full list."

[62] Just 72 hours after the Chinese government agrees to contribute a half-billion dollars to an Indonesian theme park resort project that will provide financial benefit to him personally, Trump announces that he has ordered a bailout for ZTE, a struggling cell phone manufacturer owned by the Chinese government. Trump tweets, "President Xi of China, and I, are working together to give massive Chinese phone company, ZTE, a way to get back into business, fast. Too many jobs in China lost. Commerce Department has been instructed to get it done!" Trump's family business, it turns out, has a deal to license the Trump name to the resort, which includes a golf course and hotels.

[63] As special counsel Robert Mueller's team continues to gather evidence, Trump feels the heat. He and his cohorts increase their unfounded attacks on the integrity of the investigation. Based on the revelation that the FBI used a confidential informant in 2016 as part of its counterintelligence investigation into election meddling by Russia, Trump now accuses the Obama administration of having "implanted" a "partisan spy" in his campaign in order to help Clinton. This echoes Trump's earlier unsubstantiated claim that Obama wiretapped Trump Tower. Moreover, the use of confidential informants by law enforcement is a standard investigative procedure. As a result of this latest claim, the White House calls for a meeting with Deputy Attorney General Rod Rosenstein and FBI Director Christopher Wray to learn details about the FBI's actions in this instance. At first, only Republican members of Congress are invited to attend, but Trump later relents to pressure from the other side of the aisle and schedules two separate meetings, one with Republicans and one with Democrats. The law enforcement officials involved are reluctant to have any such meetings because of their concerns over revealing confidential sources and methods.

[64] On May 24, 2018, Trump goes on television to announce his cancellation of the much touted and highly anticipated face-to-face meeting with North Korean leader Kim Jong-Un. This follows a week of diplomatic blundering by Trump administration officials and harsh recrimination from Kim. First, Vice President Mike Pence and national security advisor John Bolton leveled veiled threats at Kim. Bolton went on television and declared that the "Libya model" is the administration's goal. The Libya model refers to the agreement reached during the George W. Bush administration under which Muammar Gaddafi gave up all of his nation's nuclear weapons, only to be killed during a U.S. led bombardment of his country during the Obama

administration. On May 17, apparently recognizing this would not be an approach favored by Kim, Trump said that "[the] Libyan model isn't the model that we have at all when we're thinking of North Korea." Shortly thereafter, however, Pence went on Fox News and said that the North Korea negotiations would end "like the Libya model ended," characterizing this as a "fact" rather than a "threat." North Korea responded by calling Pence a "political dummy," a comment cited by Trump in his announcement that the summit would be canceled. Trump leaves the door open to a rescheduling of the summit "[i]f and when Kim Jong-Un chooses to engage in constructive dialogue and actions." Meanwhile, it is reported that the souvenir gold coins the White House had made for the summit are now being offered for sale at a discount.

[65] On May 24, 2018, in an Oval Office ceremony, Trump grants a posthumous pardon to African-American boxing legend Jack Johnson, who had been convicted in 1913 of violating the Mann Act, a federal law making it illegal to cross state lines with a woman "for the purpose of prostitution or debauchery, or for any other criminal purpose." Prosecution under that law was used frequently during the Jim Crow era as a device to punish miscegenation. Johnson, the first black heavyweight champion, was hounded by racists who longed for the "great white hope" who would defeat him. He served a prison term after his conviction, derailing his boxing career, and he died destitute. While the pardon is warranted and is supported by the Congressional Black Caucus, skepticism exists as to Trump's motivations, since many of his words and actions in other instances stoke racism or, at a minimum, demonstrate a lack of concern about racial injustice. This includes his continuing vilification of the Central Park Five (black youths wrongfully convicted of murdering a white girl who was jogging in the park), his baseless and shameless promotion of the idea that Barack Obama was not born in the U.S., his repeated failure to denounce the Ku Klux Klan, and his strong and relentless denunciation of black athletes for kneeling during the national anthem to protest racial injustices.

[66] On May 25, 2018, Trump delivers a commencement speech to graduating seniors at the U.S. Naval Academy in Annapolis. Not surprisingly, it is a political speech filled with self-congratulatory messages, exaggerations, and outright Trumpian lies. Among many other demonstrably false claims, Trump states, "We just got you a big pay raise, first time in 10 years." The fact is that the military has received a pay raise in each of the last 10 years and nearly every year since 1945. Military pay raises, by law, are tied to the Employment Cost Index (ECI), although a president or Congress may request more or less. This year's increase of 2.4 percent is in the mid-range of increases during the past decade, with the highest being 3.9 percent in 2009. Trump also tells the graduates, "Very soon, you're going to have 355 beautiful ships – 355. That's almost a couple hundred more ships." In fact, the number of additional ships will be 80 (increasing the fleet from 275 active ships to 355) and that increase is not expected to be achieved until the 2050s, which most people would not consider "very soon."

[67] On May 29, 2018, actress Roseanne Barr posts a tweet comparing Valerie Jarrett, an African-American and special advisor to former president Barack Obama, to an ape. Barr's television show, *Roseanne*, which quickly became a ratings hit when it was revived earlier this year, is almost immediately canceled by ABC. Robert Iger, the chairman of Disney (ABC's parent company), telephones Jarrett to apologize. Barr has been a vocal Trump supporter and plays that role on the show. Trump remains silent about Barr's racist tweet, but complains on Twitter about Iger's failure to apologize to him, presumably for the network's sometimes negative coverage of Trump's statements and actions. ABC is also home to late night host Jimmy Kimmel, who has been a critic of Trump's policies. Following cancellation of her show, Barr deletes the offensive post and issues an apology for her comments, partly blaming the post on the sleep aid Ambien. Sanofi, the maker of Ambien, responds on Twitter, "While all pharmaceutical treatments have side effects, racism is not a known side effect of any Sanofi medication." Barr has a history of strange tweets that indulge in conspiracy theories and attacks against the media.

[68] Following meetings called by the White House to investigate the FBI's use of a confidential informant in what Trump has dubbed "spygate" (see note 63), Trump's allegations of wrongdoing are publicly refuted, even by some of his supporters. Most notably, South Carolina Republican Trey Gowdy, who serves as

House Oversight Committee chairman and attended the closed-door briefing, tells Fox News that "the FBI did exactly what my fellow citizens would want them to do when they got the information they got." He later tells CBS News, "When the FBI comes into contact with information about what a foreign government may be doing in our election cycle, I think they have an obligation to run it out." Fox News legal analyst Andrew Napolitano, a favorite of the Trump administration, also says that Trump's "spy" claim appears to be "baseless" and that the FBI was engaging in "standard operating procedure." Other Trump allies, including attorney and law professor Alan Dershowitz, join this chorus. Nevertheless, Trump is not ready to abandon his "spygate" conspiracy theory. Sarah Sanders tells reporters, "The president still has concerns about whether or not the FBI acted inappropriately having people in his campaign."

[69] On June 1, 2018, Trump announces to reporters outside the White House that the summit with North Korean leader Kim Jong-Un is back on. This announcement comes shortly after Trump meets with a North Korean envoy, who has brought a letter from Kim in an oversized envelope. In remarks to the reporters, Trump characterizes the letter as "very nice" and "very interesting." He also says to them, "Oh would you like to see what was in that letter! How much? How much?" Several moments later, when he again is asked about the contents of the correspondence, he says he has not opened it yet.

[70] In recent correspondence to special counsel Robert Mueller, Trump's attorneys admit that the president did, in fact, dictate the infamous statement given to the *New York Times* last summer that characterized Donald Trump Jr.'s 2016 Trump Tower meeting with Russian officials as being primarily about adoption policies. This directly contradicts past denials by the White House. The meeting, as well as Trump's role in crafting the false statement, reportedly has been a focus of Mueller's probe into Russian interference with the 2016 presidential election. In an early morning tweet on June 4, following the revelation about his attorneys' admission, Trump asserts that he has the "absolute right" to pardon himself. In a television interview later that day, Rudy Giuliani tells CNN's Chris Cuomo, "I don't think anybody's lying. I think a mistake was made." Giuliani also supports Trump's claim of authority to self-pardon, but says Trump will not do so because of the "practical limitation" that it would constitute political suicide.

[71] On June 5, 2018, Trump holds a "Celebration of America" on the South Lawn of the White House. The event replaces the previously planned Philadelphia Eagles Super Bowl victory celebration, which Trump canceled after learning that very few members of the team were willing to attend. As a military band plays "God Bless America," Trump seems unfamiliar with the words, but gamely tries to fake it.

[72] Trump repeatedly and falsely claims that his administration's new policy of separating migrant children from their parents at the U.S.- Mexico border is the Democrats' fault. Attorney General Jeff Sessions had announced the policy in May as part of the administration's "zero tolerance" approach to unlawful immigration. Sessions defends the policy by stating that since illegal border crossings are a crime, the parents must be prosecuted and, consequently, their children must be taken from them. Under the Obama administration, such matters were handled civilly through the immigration courts, often resulting in deportation, but families were not separated. The new administration's draconian policy is sparking outrage, both domestically and abroad. The United Nations human rights office has called for an "immediate halt" to the family separation approach and many U.S. politicians and commentators have denounced it.

[73] On June 6, 2018, during a meeting of top administration officials, Vice President Mike Pence appears to mimic Trump's movements. In a video that goes viral on social media, Trump can be seen removing his plastic water bottle from a table where he is sitting, and then placing the bottle on the floor beside him. For no apparent reason, Pence then immediately does the same with his own water bottle.

[74] On June 7, 2018, when asked by a reporter in the Oval Office how he is preparing for his upcoming summit with North Korea's Kim Jong-Un, Trump responds, "I think I'm very well-prepared. I don't think I have to prepare very much. It's about attitude. It's about willingness to get things done. But I think I have been prepared for this summit for a very long time."

[75] The G-7 summit is an annual meeting of the seven major industrialized nations, which in total represent more than 60 percent of the global net worth. Economics ordinarily is the main topic of discussion, although side sessions often occur to address other global issues. The group previously included Russia (and therefore was called the G-8), but its members voted in 2014 to suspend Russia's participation due to its annexation of Crimea from Ukraine. This year's meeting, hosted by Canada, promised to be somewhat more adversarial than normal because of tariffs imposed by the Trump administration earlier this month on products from participating countries. Acrimony quickly materializes when Trump asserts that Russia should be permitted to rejoin the group and be included in the summit. Almost all other members express strong opposition to this idea. Also, Canadian Prime Minister Justin Trudeau describes as "insulting" Trump's decision to invoke national security as a justification for the tariffs. Despite their differences on trade and other issues, the summit participants prepare a "joint communique," which sets forth the agreements they have been able to reach. The communique includes a statement on the need for "free, fair, and mutually beneficial trade," a joint demand that Russia "cease with its destabilizing behavior" and withdraw its support for Syrian President Bashar al-Assad, and a pledge to "permanently" ensure that Iran's nuclear program remains peaceful. It does not include an agreement on climate issues, as Trump previously had withdrawn from the Paris climate change accord. Trump, who had arrived late to the summit, leaves before it concludes. Before departing, however, he expresses his agreement to the joint communique and promises to sign it. In a news conference at the conclusion of the summit, Trudeau vows to press ahead with retaliatory tariffs against the U.S., stating, "Canadians are polite and reasonable but we will not be pushed around." Then, in tweets while flying to his summit with Kim Jong-Un in Singapore, Trump states that he has instructed U.S. officials "not to endorse the communique as we look at tariffs on automobiles." He goes on to say that this move is based on Trudeau's "false statements… and the fact that Canada is charging massive tariffs to our US farmers, workers and companies." He also tweets that Trudeau is "[v]ery dishonest and weak." Trudeau's office responds by saying that the prime minister was only repeating what he had said before, both publicly and in private conversations with Trump.

[76] On June 12, 2018, Trump meets privately with North Korean leader Kim Jong-Un. Only interpreters are present for their conversation, which consumes over 90 minutes. This summit is accompanied by much fanfare, with pre-and post-meeting photo opportunities. Numerous pictures emerge of the two men shaking hands and Trump warmly placing his own hand on Kim's elbow and shoulder. In a press conference following the meeting, Trump claims to have formed a "very special bond" with Kim (by all previous accounts a brutal dictator who murders his political adversaries and suppresses dissent), and calls him "a very talented man" who "loves his country very much." Contrast this with Trump's disparaging characterization of his ally, the prime minister of Canada (see note 75). Trump also proudly announces, "They were willing to de-nuke." However, in a joint statement issued by the meeting participants, Kim merely "reaffirms" the same commitment to denuclearize that North Korea repeatedly has made since 1992. It also is far less specific than the Iran nuclear deal struck by the Obama administration, which resulted in Iran eliminating 98 percent of its enriched uranium and which Trump abandoned because he did not like it (and, well, it was Obama's). The vague and general joint statement contains nothing about timetables or methods for achieving denuclearization, nothing about how compliance will be verified, and no clear pledge to permanently halt testing of nuclear weapons or long-range missiles. Indeed, it contains far less detail than previous agreements with the North Korean regime that were breached. Moreover, to the shock and dismay of South Korea and Japan, Trump announces that the U.S. will suspend the joint military exercises it has been conducting for years with South Korea to help ensure stability in the region. This is a clear and significant U.S. concession in exchange for vague North Korean promises that have been made before but never kept. In his press conference, Trump praises Kim's negotiating skills. Those skills, or Trump's lack thereof, are confirmed by the results.

[77] Upon arrival home after his summit with Kim Jong-Un, Trump declares in a tweet that North Korea, which still possesses a nuclear arsenal and long-range missiles capable of reaching the U.S., is "no longer a

nuclear threat." (Incidentally, weeks later it is confirmed that North Korea has not taken steps to denuclearize and, in fact, appears to be building new ballistic missiles.)

[78] On June 14, 2018, the Justice Department's Inspector General Michael Horowitz issues his long-awaited report on the department's conduct in connection with the Hillary Clinton email investigation. The report, which is more than 500 pages long, condemns former FBI director James Comey for failing to follow department protocol when he publicly announced the investigation's conclusions and when he later disclosed that he was reopening the investigation. The report does not directly address the correctness of Comey's decision to refrain from charging Clinton, but it does conclude that political bias was not a motivating factor in that decision. The report also criticizes then Attorney General Loretta Lynch's handling of her June 2016 airport tarmac encounter with Bill Clinton and her failure to adequately manage Comey and his investigation. It finds highly problematic the anti-Trump text exchanges in 2016 between FBI agents Lisa Page and Peter Strzok, but does not conclude that their bias infected the investigation of either Clinton's emails or Russian interference in the presidential election. Notably, the report says little about special counsel Mueller's ongoing investigation into Russian interference in the election, and certainly does nothing to undermine that investigation. Lisa Page never was a member of Mueller's investigative team and Strzok was removed from the team as soon as Mueller became aware of his offending emails. None of this stops Trump from falsely telling reporters, on the White House North Lawn the day after issuance of the report, that it "totally exonerates me." Trump goes on to say, "There was no collusion. There was no obstruction. And if you read the report, you will see that." He also asserts that, based on the report, the Mueller investigation has been "discredited." Three days later, in televised testimony before the Senate Judiciary Committee, Inspector General Horowitz rebuts Trump's assertion that the report exonerates him of collusion with Russia, saying flatly, "We did not look into collusion questions." The report also does not address the obstruction issue. Further, when asked by a member of the Judiciary Committee whether he considers the Mueller investigation to be a "witch hunt" (a term Trump repeatedly uses to describe it), current FBI director Christopher Wray (a Trump appointee) says no.

[79] Feeling more heat from the unpopularity of his policy of separating families at the southern border and placing children in holding cells, Trump doubles down, employing dehumanizing terminology and racist dog whistles to describe those immigrants. Trump uses words like "infest," which conjures swarms of insects, rodents or vermin. It is reminiscent of Hitler's references to Jews, as is Trump's equating their presence to criminal hordes. He continues to blame Democrats for the fiasco he created. Attorney General Jeff Sessions, who is identified as having recommended the strategy of family separation as a means to deter border crossings, quotes the Bible as justification for using criminal prosecutions rather than the prior administration's approach of civil enforcement. In a speech to law enforcement officers in Fort Wayne, Indiana, Sessions says, "I would cite you to the Apostle Paul and his clear and wise command in Romans 13, to obey the laws of the government because God has ordained the government for his purposes." Commentators point out that this same passage was used in the 1840s and 1850s by defenders of the South or of slavery to ward off abolitionists who believed slavery to be morally wrong. In response to reporter questions about Sessions' comments, White House press secretary Sarah Sanders defends them, stating, "I can say that it is very biblical to enforce the law." Meanwhile, religious leaders condemn the administration's actions, citing other Bible verses. For example, the Vatican tweets a verse from Deuteronomy: "The Bible teaches that God 'loves the foreigner residing among you, giving them food and clothing. And you are to love those who are foreigners, for you yourselves were foreigners in Egypt' (Deuteronomy 10:18-19)." At a meeting of the U.S. Conference of Catholic Bishops, the nation's Catholic leaders strongly denounce the administration's immigration policies as immoral. One bishop even suggests that Catholics who help carry out the current zero tolerance and family separation policies are violating their faith and perhaps should be denied communion.

[80] Right wing commentators weigh in on the crisis created by the administration's policy of separating immigrant children from their parents. Ann Coulter tells Trump to ignore videos and audios of immigrant children crying because they are "child actors," Laura Ingraham says that the child detention centers are like

"summer camp," and Corey Lewandowski responds with a derisive "womp womp" when a fellow panelist discusses the fact that a 12-year old with Down Syndrome was taken away from his mother. All on Fox News, of course.

[81] On June 20, 2018, bowing to pressure from adverse publicity and numerous members of his own party, Trump signs an executive order ending the policy of separating children from their parents at the border with Mexico. Trump and his surrogates had insisted, wrongly, that his administration had no choice but to follow such a process because the law required it. He previously had said that only Congress could fix the problem, while Democrats countered that he could do it with his signature alone. In reversing his position on family separations, Trump now claims he did not like the "sight" or "feeling" of it. Trump says, however, that the administration's "zero tolerance" policy, under which it refers all illegal border crossings for criminal prosecution, will remain in effect. The Department of Homeland Security states that over 2,300 minors were separated from their families at the border between May 5, 2018, when the policy was implemented, and June 9.

[82] A day after her husband signs an executive order discontinuing his administration's family separation policy, Melania Trump visits a Texas shelter housing immigrant children victimized by that policy. Photographs show her boarding the plane to Texas wearing a green khaki jacket with the words "I REALLY DON'T CARE, DO U?" scrawled on the back. She is seen wearing the same jacket while leaving the aircraft following her return flight that evening. Despite the confusion and backlash that follows, Melania remains silent as to the intended meaning of her strange wardrobe choice for a trip that is supposed to demonstrate compassion. The former model has been careful about her attire in the past, often appearing to send a message by her choice, such as when she wore a "pussy bow" blouse after the *Access Hollywood* tape surfaced, in which her husband famously proclaimed that he could grab women "by the pussy" with impunity. Also, when Melania travels abroad, she usually chooses outfits that reflect the country she is visiting. Although the White House East Wing communications director responds to media inquiries by saying that it was "just a jacket" and there were "no hidden messages," the president later tweets that Melania's message refers to the "Fake News Media," about which "she truly no longer cares!"

[83] On June 26, 2018, the U.S. Supreme Court, in a 5-to-4 decision, upholds Trump's ban on travel from predominantly Muslim countries. It was the third iteration of Trump's ban, which he previously had derided as a "watered down" and "politically correct" version that was necessitated by decisions of lower federal courts striking down the first two versions. The Supreme Court's decision breaks down along ideological lines, with the five conservative justices voting to uphold the ban and the four liberal justices dissenting. Justice Neil Gorsuch, a conservative appointed by Trump in the early days of his administration, predictably votes with the majority. (Trump was able to appoint Gorsuch to a seat on the court after Republicans, using a strategy engineered by Senate Majority Leader Mitch McConnell, had blocked a vote on Obama nominee Merrick Garland throughout the year 2016.) Writing for the majority, Chief Justice Roberts concludes that Trump has ample executive authority to make such national security judgments to secure the nation's borders, and essentially finds Trump's history of anti-Muslim statements to be irrelevant. In a passionate dissent that she reads from the bench, Justice Sotomayor provides several examples of Trump's anti-Muslim statements as indicating the true and, in her view, unconstitutional motivation for the ban, and disparages the majority decision as being no better than *Korematsu v. United States*, a 1944 decision upholding the detention of Japanese-Americans during World War II. Trump hails the court's ruling as a "tremendous victory" and "a moment of profound vindication following months of hysterical commentary from the media and Democratic politicians who refuse to do what it takes to secure our border and our country." One day after the travel ban decision is announced, Justice Anthony Kennedy, who occasionally broke with the conservative wing of the court and therefore was a crucial swing vote, issues a statement that he will retire at the end of July. This leaves Trump another opportunity to appoint a staunch conservative like Gorsuch and shape the court for generations to come.

[84] On June 28, 2018, Deputy Attorney General Rod Rosenstein and FBI Director Christopher Wray appear before the House Judiciary Committee to answer questions about how their departments handled the Hillary Clinton email investigation. Representative Jim Jordan, a Tea Party Republican from Ohio, accuses Rosenstein of withholding information from Congress and failing to comply with the committee's subpoenas. The exchange becomes heated, with Rosenstein denying Jordan's allegations, defending his department, and objecting to the hostile and personal tone of Jordan's questions. At one point, Jordan accusingly asks Rosenstein whether he had threatened to subpoena the "telephone calls" of House Intelligence Committee members. Applause erupts when Rosenstein sarcastically replies, "There's no way to subpoena phone calls." Representative Trey Gowdy of South Carolina, another Tea Party conservative, grills Rosenstein about special counsel Robert Mueller's investigation into Russian interference with the 2016 election. He accuses Rosenstein, Mueller's boss, of allowing the one-year old probe to continue, angrily demanding that he "finish it the hell up, because this country is being torn apart." Gowdy famously led the congressional investigation into the Obama administration's handling of the fatal terrorist attack on the U.S. Embassy in Benghazi, a probe that consumed more than two years and uncovered no new information other than the existence of Hillary Clinton's private email server. The behavior of Jordan, Gowdy and other Republicans on the Judiciary Committee is part of their continuing effort to discredit the Justice Department and Mueller's investigators, furthering Trump's assertion that they are biased against him. Neither Rosenstein nor Wray are Democrats, and Wray is a Trump appointee.

[85] On July 5, 2018, after months of adverse publicity due to misconduct allegations, Scott Pruitt resigns from his position as Environmental Protection Agency (EPA) administrator. The allegations included spending taxpayer funds for first class air travel and for excessive personal security, entering into an inappropriate transaction with a lobbyist, inappropriately directing his driver to use a siren to allow smoother transition through traffic, and improperly using his influence to secure his wife a high-paying government job. Pruitt, carrying out Trump's wishes, had pursued an aggressive policy of dismantling EPA programs and regulations, especially those created during the Obama administration.

[86] As Trump's massive tariffs on Chinese imports to the U.S. go into effect, satirist Andy Borowitz of *The New Yorker* doesn't miss a beat. He pens a wonderful piece entitled, "China Slaps Two-Thousand Percent Tariff on Tanning Beds." As an additional retaliatory measure in the escalating trade war, Borowitz writes that China has "placed a four-thousand percent tariff on all spray-tan products headed for the U.S., as well as instant-tanning lotions, makeup foundation, and several popular hues of orange paint, including butter rum and burnt sienna." Borowitz has White House press secretary Sarah Sanders characterizing these moves as an "act of war."

[87] As Trump's one-on-one meeting with Russian President Vladimir Putin approaches, he continues to have only words of praise for the corrupt and murderous dictator. Trump also continues to avoid acknowledging Russia's efforts to sway the 2016 presidential election in his favor, despite evidence of such tampering sufficient to convince the entire U.S. intelligence community and the bipartisan Senate Intelligence Committee. At the same time, Trump does Russia's bidding by, among other things, denigrating NATO and its member nations, advocating for the suspension of Russia's G-7 membership to be lifted, and defending Putin's forced annexation of Crimea. Through the special counsel investigation into Russia's election meddling and the indictments resulting from that probe, more details arise concerning the substantial connections between Trump campaign and administration officials and Russian oligarchs. Additionally, Trump's own historical ties to Russia, both personal and financial, come into sharper focus, including his heavy reliance on Russian oligarchs to bail his businesses out of actual or impending bankruptcy. As Trump continues to behave like a Russian asset, we are left wondering whether he was carefully selected and recruited to serve that role.

[88] On July 12, 2018, FBI agent Peter Strzok is grilled by members of the House Judiciary Committee and House Oversight and Government Reform Committee concerning his actions and anti-Trump text messages while investigating the Hillary Clinton emails and Russia's election interference. The proceedings are highly

partisan, with Republican members attempting to establish that Strzok's political views infected those investigations and, ultimately, tainted the Mueller probe as well. The show is part of a continuing effort by House Republicans to support Trump's claim that the investigations of Russian meddling are a "witch hunt" promoted by an anti-Trump "deep state." Strzok, who was removed from the Mueller team after discovery of the text messages, strongly maintains that his personal political views had no impact on his professional conduct as an investigator and certainly did not affect the outcome of those investigations. He points out the generally conservative bent of the FBI as well as its internal checks and balances. He notes that he had a major role in the FBI's Russian interference probe, where the agency chose not to publicly disclose its concerns prior to the election, a decision that benefited Trump. Democrats use the committee hearing to demonstrate the hypocrisy of the Republican attack on the integrity of the investigations, introducing similar anti-Trump statements made by high-ranking Republicans before his nomination. The day after this hearing, Deputy Attorney General Rod Rosenstein announces a new indictment stemming from the Mueller investigation. The 29-page indictment names 12 Russian intelligence officers and provides great detail as to the nature of their election interference, including hacking of Hillary Clinton's email accounts and Democratic National Committee computer networks, using conduits such as WikiLeaks to publish the information illegally obtained, money laundering, and attempting to break into state elections boards. The indictment also describes an online conversation between the Russian operatives and a "person who was in regular contact with senior members of the presidential campaign of Donald J. Trump." People familiar with the case identify that person as Roger Stone, a longtime friend and advisor to Trump. On the same day as the new indictment is announced, Trump has a stopover in Great Britain on his way to Helsinki, Finland for a one-on-one meeting with Russian President Vladimir Putin. Apparently without knowledge of or regard for protocol, Trump clumsily walks in front of Queen Elizabeth while reviewing her honor guard. Trump also criticizes Great Britain's Prime Minister Theresa May for allegedly failing to heed his advice concerning Brexit (Britain's withdrawal from the European Union), saying that her approach had likely "killed" any chance of a new trade deal with the U.S. once Brexit is complete. In a later joint press conference Trump tries to walk back that criticism. Then, in a televised interview from Scotland on July 14, 2018, Trump names the European Union as a "foe" of the United States because of "what they do to us in trade." With all of this as prelude, and still tweeting that the Mueller probe of Russian interference with the U.S. election is a witch hunt, Trump boards a plane for his meeting with Putin. Commentators express concern about Trump's motives for the meeting and the fact that it will be held in private.

[89] During an interview with British television host Piers Morgan before leaving for his meeting with Putin, Trump is asked what incentive the U.S. has to "do a great deal with the United Kingdom." The question is an important one in light of Trump's recent derogatory statements about a post-Brexit trade deal (see note 88). Demonstrating his lack of knowledge concerning geopolitics and in his usual inarticulate manner, Trump responds, "We would make a great deal with the United Kingdom because they have product that we like. I mean they have a lot of great product. They make phenomenal things, you know, and you have different names – you can say 'England,' you can say 'United Kingdom.' So many different – you know you have, you have so many different names – 'Great Britain.' I always say: 'Which one do you prefer? Great Britain?' You understand what I'm saying?"

[90] On July 16, 2018, Trump meets behind closed doors with Russian President Putin for approximately two hours, with interpreters being the only other persons present. At a press conference following the meeting, Trump again refuses to support the conclusion of U.S. intelligence agencies that Russia interfered with the 2016 presidential election in an effort to help him and defeat Hillary Clinton. Trump's current equivocation on the subject comes despite the recently announced indictment of 12 high-ranking Russian operatives and the detailed description of their activities. Trump states that in their private meeting Putin gave him "an extremely strong and powerful" denial. When asked during the news conference whether he believes U.S. intelligence or Putin, Trump responds, "They said they think it's Russia. I have President Putin; he just said it's not Russia. ... I will say this: I don't see any reason why it would be." In response to a reporter's question, Putin admits he wanted Trump to win the 2016 election, stating that it was "because [Trump] talked about normalizing relations" between their two countries. In a tweet just before the closed door

meeting with Putin, Trump had said, "Our relationship with Russia has NEVER been worse thanks to many years of U.S. foolishness and stupidity and now, the Rigged Witch Hunt!" The Russian foreign ministry retweeted this, adding "We agree." At the news conference, Trump repeats his assertion that the U.S. shares responsibility for the breakdown in relations with Russia and states that, "as of four hours ago," that relationship is changing.

[91] Trump's comments and actions during the summit with Putin draw strong rebuke back home, even from Republicans. Senator John McCain provides the harshest criticism from a member of Trump's own party, calling Trump's joint news conference with Putin "one of the most disgraceful performances by an American president in memory." McCain goes on to say, "The damage inflicted by President Trump's naivete, egotism, false equivalence and sympathy for autocrats is difficult to calculate. But it is clear that the summit in Helsinki was a tragic mistake." He adds, "No prior president has ever abased himself more abjectly before a tyrant." House Speaker Paul Ryan says, "There is no question that Russia interfered in our election and continues attempts to undermine democracy here and around the world. … The president must appreciate that Russia is not our ally. There is no moral equivalence between the United States and Russia, which remains hostile to our most basic values and ideals." Senate Majority Leader Mitch McConnell tells reporters, "As I've said repeatedly, the Russians are not our friends and I entirely agree with the assessment of our intelligence community." Senate Foreign Relations Committee Chairman Bob Corker comments that Trump's performance "made us look, as a nation, like a pushover." He further states, "I did not think this was a good moment for our country" and "I would guess [Putin's] having caviar right now." Senator Ben Sasse calls Trump's claim that both the U.S. and Russia are responsible for the deterioration of their relationship "bizarre and flat-out wrong." Sasse also says, "America wants a good relationship with the Russian people but Vladimir Putin and his thugs are responsible for Soviet-style aggression. When the president plays these moral equivalency games, he gives Putin a propaganda win he desperately needs." Senator Jeff Flake tweets, "I never thought I would see the day when our American President would stand on the stage with the Russian President and place blame on the United States for Russian aggression. This is shameful." Mitt Romney, the 2012 Republican presidential nominee, tweets, "President Trump's decision to side with Putin over American intelligence agencies is disgraceful and detrimental to our democratic principles. Russia remains our number one geopolitical adversary; claiming a moral equivalence between the United States and Russia not only defies reason and history, it undermines our national integrity and impairs our global credibility." Representative Will Hurd, a former CIA officer, tweets, "I've seen Russian intelligence manipulate many people over my professional career and I never would have thought that the U.S. President would become one of the ones getting played by old KGB hands." Even former House Speaker Newt Gingrich, a staunch Trump supporter, chimes in, calling it "the most serious mistake of his presidency" and stating that it "must be corrected immediately." These are just a few of the many negative comments from Trump's fellow Republicans. For their part, Democrats not only deride Trump's performance, but openly speculate about his motivations and what personal, financial or political leverage Putin might have over him. In addition, there is speculation and concern about what other things Trump might have said and conceded during his private session with Putin. Senator Mark Warner asks, "If the President cannot defend the United States and its interests in public, how can we trust him to stand up for our country in private?"

[92] On July 18, 2018, apparently in response to the onslaught of criticism from members of his own party (see note 91), Trump attempts to retreat from his position that the U.S. intelligence community was wrong in its assessment of Russian meddling. Arms crossed and slowly reading from a prepared statement, he now grudgingly agrees that Russia tried to interfere with the election, but then departs from the script and adds the contradictory (and factually unsupported) statement that it "could be other people also." Trump unconvincingly tries to walk back his comment from the joint press conference with Putin, where he said, "I don't see any reason why it would be [Russia]." He now claims he misspoke, seemingly blaming a reluctance to use bad grammar: "The sentence should have been, 'I don't see any reason why it *wouldn't* be Russia.' Sort of a double negative."

[93] In a press briefing on July 18, 2018, White House press secretary Sarah Sanders confirms that Trump is still considering what he described in Helsinki as Russian President Vladimir Putin's "incredible offer," in which Putin would grant special counsel Robert Mueller access to interview the recently indicted Russian operatives in exchange for Russia conducting interviews of 11 U.S. citizens. Putin's list of proposed interviewees includes former U.S. ambassador to Russia Michael McFaul and businessman Bill Browder. Both McFaul and Browder have been strong critics of Putin's policies and human rights abuses. The Kremlin has accused Browder of committing tax fraud and illegally contributing $400,000 to Hillary Clinton's campaign, allegations which appear to be baseless. Russian state media claims that McFaul is wanted in connection with the investigation of Browder. Browder is a particular object of Putin's ire because of the revelations of Putin's corrupt and brutal practices contained in Browder's book, *Red Notice*, and the fact that Browder was instrumental in securing passage of the Magnitsky Act, under which Congress froze the assets of numerous high-level Russian officials suspected of committing human rights abuses. This legislation, along with similar approaches implemented by other nations, is believed to have seriously impacted foreign assets tied to much of Putin's personal wealth. The law, which was enacted in 2012, is named for Browder's former tax accountant, Sergei Magnitsky, who Browder alleges was jailed and beaten to death after uncovering a multi-million dollar tax fraud scheme involving close Putin associates. Putin has made repeal of the Magnitsky Act a high priority. In the infamous Trump Tower meeting with Donald Trump Jr. and Paul Manafort in the summer of 2016 (arranged for the ostensible purpose of disclosing dirt on Hillary Clinton to the Trump campaign), Russian lawyer Natalia Veselnitskaya, a Kremlin operative, seized the opportunity to lobby for Magnitsky Act repeal. Trump's comments about the "incredible offer" of a witness exchange and Sanders' affirmation that it is still under discussion brings sharp and almost universal rebuke from both Democrats and Republicans. Even Heather Nauert, the spokesperson for Trump's State Department, calls Russia's allegations against Browder "absurd" and labels the prospect of Russia interviewing a former U.S. diplomat a "grave concern." On July 19, 2018, the day after Sanders' press briefing, the Senate passes a unanimous (98 to zero) resolution against turning over U.S. citizens to Russia for interview. Although the resolution is non-binding, it sends a clear message. Shortly before the resolution's result is announced, the administration states that while Putin's offer was a "sincere" one, the President does not agree with it.

[94] At the Tony Awards on June 10, 2018, Oscar-winning actor Robert DeNiro, a frequent Trump critic, introduces Bruce Springsteen's musical performance by saying, with fists pumped, "It's no longer 'down with Trump,' it's 'fuck Trump.'" DeNiro receives a standing ovation and the moment goes viral on social media. Needless to say, Trump and his supporters are not pleased.

[95] In a speech, Iranian President Hassan Rouhani declares: "America should know that peace with Iran is the mother of all peace, and war with Iran is the mother of all wars." Trump responds with an all capital letters (i.e., shouting) tweet containing his own "demented words of violence and death."

[96] At a briefing for reporters, White House press secretary Sarah Sanders announces that Trump is "exploring the mechanisms" to remove security clearances from former CIA Director John Brennan plus five other former top national security officials: James Comey, James Clapper, Michael Hayden, Susan Rice and Andrew McCabe. Sanders accuses these officials of having "politicized and in some cases monetized their public service and security clearances" by "making baseless accusations of improper contact with Russia or being influenced by Russia." What all of the listed individuals have in common is their public criticism of Trump and his policies. While there is some debate about whether Trump has the authority to revoke security clearances based on political criticism and protected speech, most commentators agree that it is unprecedented and morally repugnant. Incidentally, the clearances of Comey and McCabe already had been revoked due to their terminations from the FBI. Furthermore, there is great irony in the Trump administration complaining about "monetizing" public service. Less than a month after Sanders' disclosure about Trump's consideration of revoking security clearances, Trump begins following through by removing Brennan's clearance.

[97] On July 24, 2018, CNN discloses the contents of a recording secretly made by Trump's longtime legal counsel Michael Cohen, in which the two of them discuss buying the silence of former *Playboy* model Karen McDougal, with whom Trump allegedly had an extramarital affair. The recorded meeting occurred just weeks before the 2016 presidential election. Trump previously had denied any knowledge of such hush money discussions or transactions. Cohen's offices were raided by federal investigators in April (see note 59) and he now is in jeopardy of criminal prosecution for bank fraud and campaign finance violations. Statements and conduct by Cohen in recent weeks demonstrate that he is upset with Trump, as the president appears to be distancing himself from the once fiercely loyal attorney and fixer. In response to disclosure of the recording, Trump tweets, "What kind of lawyer would tape a client? So sad!"

[98] In a speech at the White House on July 27, 2018, Trump declares that the Commerce Department's 4.1 percent U.S. gross domestic product (GDP) growth figure for the second quarter of 2018 is "an economic turnaround of historic proportions." He also calls the economic growth figures "amazing." Not surprisingly, given Trump's penchant for hyperbole, it is neither historic nor amazing, nor does it demonstrate an economic turnaround. This one quarter figure was exceeded four times during the Obama administration, 12 times during the Clinton administration, and 13 times during the Reagan administration. Further, most economists agree that the current quarterly increase in GDP was fueled, in part, by a temporary surge in exports (particularly soybeans to China) as other countries sought to stockpile goods in anticipation of Trump's announced tariffs. As for Trump taking credit for an economic turnaround, experts point out that the U.S. economy has been growing steadily since June 2009, the second-longest period of expansion on record. In his speech, Trump also predicts, without basis, that the 4.1 percent growth rate for the single quarter is "very, very sustainable." Most economists predict the opposite, saying that the figure will be difficult to replicate and is likely to move much lower, probably leading to a recession. In support of his claim of an unprecedented turnaround, Trump additionally argues that job growth is on the rise during his administration. While this is true, he fails to note that the rate of job growth during his first 18 months in office (a monthly average of 193,000 new jobs) is less than it was during the last 18 months of the Obama administration (a monthly average of 206,000 new jobs).

[99] At political rallies, to frenzied cheering from his base, Trump continues to deride the press as the "real enemy of the people" and to call most mainstream coverage of his presidency "fake news." He renews this assault on free press with a vengeance after the generally negative coverage of his summit with Russian President Putin. As a result of the anti-press atmosphere he stokes, many reporters fall victim to verbal abuse and threats of physical violence. In late July 2018, *New York Times* publisher A.G. Sulzberger meets with Trump to air concerns about his attacks on journalists, including not only the safety issues it raises for those professionals but also the fact that such negative branding by the leader of the free world provides license for despots to persecute news media, silence critics and evade accountability. Apparently this plea has no impact, as Trump promptly resumes and intensifies the same rhetoric.

[100] Professional basketball star LeBron James becomes the latest black athlete to incur Trump's wrath for criticizing him. While being interviewed on CNN by Don Lemon, who also is black, James expresses the uncontroversial opinion that Trump is divisive and emboldens racists. Trump's subsequent tweet, branding both James and Lemon as unintelligent, more than proves the point James has made. (As a throwaway line, the tweet includes the statement that Trump prefers former basketball star Michael Jordan to James.) In the recent past, Trump repeatedly has referred to Maxine Waters, one of the most prominent African-American members of Congress and a vocal Trump critic, as "a seriously low IQ person." Of course, there are also his racially charged derogatory statements about Mexicans, his unrelenting attacks on black football players for kneeling in protest of racial inequality during the national anthem, his reluctance to denounce the Ku Klux Klan and other white nationalist organizations, and many other examples plainly demonstrating his racial prejudices. Trump's offensive tweet about James and Lemon is immediately condemned by numerous journalists, athletes and political figures. Even Trump's wife Melania follows up with a statement supportive of James, saying that it "looks like LeBron James is working to do good things on behalf of our next generation." James recently had been celebrated in the news (and in fact was on Lemon's show) for

opening a school for at-risk children in his home town of Akron, Ohio. Called the "I Promise School," it is funded by James' non-profit organization. By contrast, Trump's non-profit foundation appears to fund no charitable causes, but instead supports Trump's personal legal settlements and art purchases.

[101] In what is shaping up to be the hottest summer on record, wildfires ravage California. Trump, a frequent climate change denier, blames the fires on "bad" environmental legislation allegedly resulting in water supplies inadequate to fight the blazes. He also asserts that water needed for firefighting is being "diverted into the Pacific Ocean." All of this is blatantly false. In response to Trump's claims, officials from the California Department of Forestry and Fire Protection, also known as Cal Fire, point out that water supplies to fight these fires has been more than sufficient and, with major reservoirs and bodies of water near the worst fire zones, easily accessible. As for Trump's statement about water "diversion" being a problem, it is conceivable that he is confused by demands for more irrigation water from Republican office-holders in California's San Joaquin Valley (among them, Trump devotee and protector Devin Nunes). Notably, water is not being "diverted" to the Pacific Ocean. It flows there from its source in the mountains, a natural phenomenon most people learn about by fifth grade. It is the San Joaquin Valley agricultural interests who are requesting diversion of more water to their fields. This complex dispute over water rights has been going on for years, but has nothing to do with the amount of water available to fight wildfires. Finally, Trump's tweet also calls for trees to be cleared. It is unclear exactly what Trump is proposing in this regard. Strategic clearing of brush and trees often is used as one course of action to contain a fire, including the ones currently being fought. Trump's statement might, however, be intended as support for more commercial logging in protected wilderness areas, an agenda his administration is pursuing. While this would provide a boon to logging companies, it is not a solution to the wildfire issue.

[102] The Trump administration proposes a new branch of the military, which Trump has dubbed "Space Force," to be added by the year 2020. It would be on a par with the Army, Navy, Air Force, Marines and Coast Guard. A new military branch only can be formed with the approval of Congress. In a speech on August 9, 2018, Vice President Pence asks Congress for an appropriation of $8 billion over five years for space security systems, but a Space Force itself is likely to cost far more. The asserted reason for establishing a new military branch dedicated to outer space is to meet galactic threats from Russia and China in the event that they develop weapons to jam, blind or destroy U.S. satellite communications systems. A space command consisting of approximately 30,000 people already exists within the Air Force and is tasked, among other things, with protecting satellites. Shortly after Pence's speech, Trump's 2020 re-election campaign manager emails supporters stating that "a new line of gear" containing Space Force insignia will be sold and asking that they vote on six possible logos.

[103] Omarosa Manigault Newman, a former top-level aide in the Trump administration, takes to the airwaves to promote her soon to be published book titled *Unhinged*. The book purports to be a behind-the-scenes expose of Trump, based on interactions spanning from Omarosa's time as a recurring contestant on Trump's reality show *The Apprentice* through the presidential campaign and the first year of the administration. During her time in the White House, Omarosa had the high-ranking title "assistant to the president" with a salary of $179,700 per year. While serving in that role, she publicly touted Trump and he called her smart and talented. All of that changed after Omarosa was fired by chief of staff John Kelly in December 2017. Omarosa, who had been the only African-American official in the White House, now says that Trump is a racist and a misogynist while Trump counters that she is "a loser," "vicious," "wacky," "not smart," and a "dog." Omarosa, who learned well the dark arts of opportunism, self-promotion and shady dealing during her long apprenticeship with Trump, states that she has secretly recorded White House conversations that support allegations contained in her book. As part of her pre-publication media blitz, she releases some of these recordings, including one of her firing by Kelly in the White House situation room and one of a subsequent conversation with the president in which he expressed surprise and dismay about her firing. She also claims to have heard a tape-recording of Trump repeatedly using the "n-word" during production of *The Apprentice*. Clearly upset by someone using his own tactics so effectively against him, Trump lashes out in a Twitter storm, only part of which is reproduced here. Through his spokesperson

Sarah Sanders, Trump contends that Omarosa's surreptitious recording of conversations proves her lack character and integrity. Omarosa responds that she did it for protection, knowing that she would be vilified if she revealed the truth about Trump.

[104] While appearing on NBC's *Meet the Press*, Trump lawyer Rudy Giuliani attempts to defend his position that Trump should not sit for an interview with special counsel Mueller because it would be a "perjury trap." Giuliani asserts, "And when you tell me that, you know, he should testify because he's going to tell the truth and he shouldn't worry, well that's so silly because it's somebody's version of the truth. Not the truth." When the show's host, Chuck Todd, interjects that "truth is truth," Giuliani responds, "No, truth isn't truth. Truth isn't truth." This comment is reminiscent of White House spokesperson Kellyanne Conway's televised response in 2017 when challenged about Sean Spicer lying in press briefings on behalf of Trump, where she famously replied that Spicer was only offering "alternative facts."

[105] In yet another delusional tweet, Trump compares special counsel Robert Mueller to the late communist-hunting demagogue Joseph McCarthy. This comes as Trump is lashing out about reports that White House counsel Donald McGahn has been cooperating with the Mueller investigation.

[106] Within moments of each other on the afternoon of August 21, 2018, a federal jury in Virginia finds Trump's former campaign manager Paul Manafort guilty of eight felony counts in the first trial related to the Mueller investigation, while in New York Trump's former lawyer and fixer Michael Cohen pleads guilty to eight felony counts as well. Manafort stands convicted of tax and bank fraud charges, and faces a second trial in another federal court on additional charges more closely related to his role in the Trump campaign. Throughout Manafort's trial, Trump attacked the prosecution in tweets and public statements, calling Mueller's team a "disgrace," repeatedly branding the Mueller investigation as a "rigged witch hunt," and referring to Manafort as a "very good person." Even after the verdict's announcement, Trump reiterates his "good man" characterization of Manafort, increasing speculation about a potential pardon as a hedge against the beleaguered defendant "flipping" and offering cooperation to Mueller's investigators. For his part, Cohen pleads guilty to criminal tax evasion and campaign finance violations. The campaign finance counts concern his unreported hush money payments to porn star Stormy Daniels and *Playboy* model Karen McDougal in an effort to influence the election. Cohen tells the judge under oath that those payments were made in coordination with and at the direction of Trump, thus implicating his former client in the crimes. Trump gives no immediate public response to Cohen's allegation but is reported to be privately seething.

[107] In a television interview on *Fox & Friends*, Trump bemoans Michael Cohen's guilty plea, claiming he lied to prosecutors to obtain a better deal for himself. Trump complains that becoming a cooperating witness for the government in exchange for more lenient treatment is something he has seen "many times" and that it is "not a fair thing." "It's called flipping and it almost ought to be illegal," he says. This is the same complaint mafia bosses have voiced about subordinates who turn on them when targeted in a criminal investigation.

[108] On August 23, 2018, just two days after the Manafort convictions and the Cohen guilty pleas (see note 106), it is revealed that David Pecker, a long-time Trump friend and ally, has been given immunity against self-incrimination by federal prosecutors. Pecker is a key witness in the investigation into payments made by the Trump campaign in 2016 to Stormy Daniels and Karen McDougal in an effort to silence them concerning alleged sexual liaisons with Trump. Pecker is the chairman of America Media, Inc., the nation's largest publisher of tabloid newspapers, including the *National Enquirer*, which strongly supported Trump's candidacy and purchased exclusive rights to McDougal's story then buried it. Pecker is rumored to have stored numerous documents concerning potentially shady transactions involving Trump in a safe in his office. The agreement to grant him immunity implies that he is cooperating with prosecutors.

[109] On August 24, 2018, a day after the revelation about David Pecker (see note 108), the *Wall Street Journal* reports that Allen Weisselberg, who has served for decades as chief financial officer for the Trump Organization, also has been granted immunity by federal prosecutors and subpoenaed to testify before a grand jury earlier this year. Although he reportedly has spoken with investigators, it is unclear whether he

yet has appeared before the grand jury. Moreover, the scope of the questioning is unknown. The *Wall Street Journal* characterizes Weisselberg as Trump's longtime "financial gatekeeper" and states that after Trump was elected, "he handed control of his financial assets and business interests to his two adult sons and Mr. Weisselberg."

[110] On August 25, 2018, Senator John McCain of Arizona succumbs to his battle with brain cancer. In the preceding months Trump and McCain had clashed openly and repeatedly, with McCain casting the deciding vote against repeal of the Affordable Care Act and taking Trump to task for his conduct at the summit with Russian president Putin. Even before those fights, Trump seemed to have a low opinion of McCain, going so far as to dismiss his military service and heroism during several years of captivity in North Vietnam. During an interview in July 2015, Trump said of McCain, "He's not a war hero. He's a war hero only because he was captured. I like people who weren't captured." In the aftermath of McCain's death, Trump opts for pettiness over protocol. Instead of following the advice of senior level White House staff to issue a public statement praising McCain for his service to the country, Trump at first limits his comments to a terse tweet of condolences to the family, with no mention of McCain himself. In accordance with tradition, other flags in Washington, D.C. and around the country are flown at half-staff until the funeral, but Trump orders the White House flag to be restored to full-staff after one day. The almost universal response to Trump's show of disrespect is negative, even from conservative media outlets. What ultimately appears to change Trump's approach, however, is a statement issued by the national commander of the American Legion, which says, "I strongly urge you to make an appropriate presidential proclamation noting Senator McCain's death and legacy of service to our nation, and that our nation's flag be half-staffed through his internment." On August 27, 2018, after this backlash, Trump issues a more robust statement expressing appreciation for McCain's service and re-lowers the flag pending McCain's funeral.

[111] Apparently feeling the walls of the Mueller investigation closing in, particularly concerning his multiple attempts to obstruct the probe, Trump engages in an ever more frantic attack on intelligence agencies, the Department of Justice and the press. In yet another outrageous early morning tweet on August 30, 2018, Trump makes the palpably false claim that NBC News anchor Lester Holt "fudged" the tape of a televised interview more than a year earlier in which Trump off-handedly admitted having fired Comey because he was looking into the campaign's potential collusion with Russia. The full unedited version of Holt's interview was made available online to the public immediately after it occurred. Perhaps finally understanding the significance of this admission in the obstruction case, Trump now implicitly resorts to denying he said what he said. This is a familiar tack for him, having previously floated the notion that the *Access Hollywood* ("grab them by the pussy") tape also might have been doctored. Further, a month before his attempt to brand the Holt interview tape as "fake news," Trump said in a speech before the Veterans of Foreign Wars, "Just remember: what you're seeing and what you're reading is not what's happening." This statement was eerily reminiscent of George Orwell's description of a totalitarian government's ultimate demand of its subjects in his novel *1984*: "The party told you to reject the evidence of your eyes and ears. It was their final, most essential command."

[112] John McCain had planned his funeral in advance as a celebration of bipartisanship and civility as well as a rebuke to Trump. Trump is not invited. While numerous political leaders from the United States and around the world gather to celebrate and eulogize McCain, including former presidents George W. Bush and Barack Obama, Trump plays golf at his Virginia resort. During her emotional eulogy, McCain's daughter Meghan takes a number of jabs at the current president. She says, "We gather here to mourn the passing of American greatness. The real thing, not cheap rhetoric from men who will never come near the sacrifice he gave so willingly, nor the opportunistic appropriation of those who lived lives of comfort and privilege." In a thinly veiled attack on Trump's slogan, she declares, "The America of John McCain has no need to be made great again because America was always great." Later, in apparent response, Trump tweets and retweets, all in capital letters, "MAKE AMERICA GREAT AGAIN!"

[113] On September 3, 2018, Trump levels yet another tweeting attack against Attorney General Jeff Sessions, this time suggesting that the Justice Department should not have brought indictments against two Republican congressmen before the November midterm elections. Representative Duncan Hunter of California had been charged in August with lavish expenditure of campaign funds for personal items and falsifying reports to the federal government concerning political finances. Representative Chris Collins of New York had been charged two weeks earlier for insider trading and lying to the FBI. Duncan and Collins were the first members of Congress to endorse Trump in his presidential bid. Trump's sarcastic castigation of Sessions not only is seen as egregious interference with federal law enforcement but also is, unsurprisingly, incorrect on the facts. Contrary to Trump's assertion, neither of these investigations was a "long running Obama era" matter. Collins was indicted for conduct occurring in 2017. While the investigation of Hunter was begun in 2016 by the Federal Election Commission, the FBI first conducted a search of Hunter's office in February 2017, after Trump took office.

[114] Within the space of 24 hours, the *Washington Post* previews revelations from Bob Woodward's new book entitled *Fear* and the *New York Times* publishes an anonymous op-ed piece purporting to have been written by a currently serving "senior administration official," both sounding the consistent theme that White House insiders consider Trump ignorant, erratic, amoral and unfit to serve as president. Both the book and the op-ed paint a picture of close advisors repeatedly having to derail Trump's worst instincts, sometimes through subterfuge, in the interests of preventing actions potentially dangerous to the country. These revelations are consistent with but significantly add to the detail contained in the Michael Wolff's book, *Fire and Fury*, published earlier in the year (see note 16). Trump is enraged by these publications. He demands that the op-ed author be outed by the *New York Times* and "turned over to the government," claiming that it is a matter of national security. Meanwhile, Senator Rand Paul suggests that White House staffers submit to a polygraph test as a means to discover the culprit's identity.

[115] In a Twitter video, Trump thanks Hurricane Florence first responders, stating, "This is a tough hurricane, one of the wettest we've ever seen from the standpoint of water."

[116] While confirmation hearings involving Supreme Court nominee Brett Kavanaugh are nearing a close, press reports reveal allegations that he had engaged in a sexual assault decades earlier. Christine Blasey Ford, a college professor, made the accusation in a confidential letter to a local legislator in early July, who shortly thereafter turned the letter over to California Senator Dianne Feinstein. The letter was leaked to the press two months later. Ford alleges that during a high school party Kavanaugh threw her onto a bed, pinned her down with his body, attempted to remove her clothing, and held his hand over her mouth when she tried to scream. Ford apparently never reported the incident to the police, but several years later did discuss it with her therapist. She also took and passed a polygraph test concerning the allegations. While senators debate how to handle these allegations in the confirmation hearings, Trump weighs in on Twitter, ignorantly questioning Ford's veracity based on her failure to file charges when the assault occurred. Republican Senator Susan Collins calls Trump's tweet "appalling," noting that most sexual assaults on women go unreported due to fear of humiliation and defeat in the criminal justice system and vilification by those (usually men) who would doubt such claims. Trump himself has been accused of sexual assault by numerous women.

ABOUT THE AUTHOR

Bob Stone is retired attorney living in Los Angeles, California. He is a graduate of Wesleyan University in Connecticut and Boston University School of Law. Other than the practice of law, his only skills are lifeguarding and writing limericks. Since his aging body is no longer compatible with saving lives or wearing a speedo, he has concluded that it is more sensible to spend his spare time and energy composing doggerel. He continues to hope that despite the efforts of the current White House administration, his children and grandchildren will be able to inhabit a safer, healthier, and more tolerant world.

Photo by Lee Whittam

ABOUT THE ILLUSTRATOR

Chris Critelli resides in New York City, where he balances his time between acting, whether it's voicing cartoons or getting beat up by superheroes, writing and drawing all kinds of stuff, and worrying about the continued survival of our democracy. But hopefully that last part will change soon. For more, find him at www.chriscritelli.com.

Photo by Aaron Phillips

Made in the USA
San Bernardino, CA
21 June 2019